For the World's Best
DRIVER

First published in Great Britain in 2010

Prion Books
an imprint of the
Carlton Publishing Group
20 Mortimer Street
London W1T 3JW

A catalogue record for this book is available
from the British Library

ISBN 978-1-85375-765-5

Printed in the UK by CPI Mackays,
Chatham, ME5 8TD

For the World's Best
DRIVER

A Glovebox-full of Fun for the Expert behind the Wheel

Mike Haskins and Clive Whichelow

Contents

Introduction

You've probably been wondering how long it would take for those around you to notice that you are in fact the world's best driver, and now at last, here is the official recognition.

You may not be the world's fastest driver – that accolade probably belongs to Lewis Hamilton or Jenson Button or one of those guys – but then you don't get the opportunity to get close to breaking the sound barrier when you're stuck in traffic crawling to work in the morning.

You may not even be the world's safest driver. You may have had the odd little shunt here and there (the other person's fault naturally); you may have once or twice exceeded the speed limit. All right, you've probably exceeded the speed limit virtually every day of your driving life, but then who hasn't? If you were the only mug going at 29 mph you'd probably have had even more shunts.

No, being the world's best driver involves other qualities. Like one of those little old ladies you've never heard of who suddenly gets awarded the OBE one day for all the quiet charity work she's done over a lifetime, you are now being officially being recognised as The World's Best Driver. Yes, you've been awarded the WBD.

You've endured road rage, back seat drivers, parking rage, and abuse from cyclists, as well as various children, dogs, and elderly passengers despoiling your lovely air-freshened interior. You've put up with squeegee merchants, charity collectors in bizarre animal costumes, parking tickets, wheel-clamps and stroppy handwritten notes placed under your windscreen wipers. You've been ripped off by garages and mechanics, patronized by sales staff, breathalysed, had your radio nicked, your aerial bent, been stuck in snow drifts, navigated through fog, and traversed fjords, level crossings, and boggy country lanes. You've crawled behind tractors, hearses, funs runs, and little old ladies doing 15 mph (on a motorway). In short, you're a hero.

Despite all this, not once have you lost your temper, run over a pedestrian, or ripped down your fluffy dice in frustration. Well, you might have done, and you may even have muttered a few choice words under your breath once or twice, but even a newly sanctified saint would be hard pressed to keep his cool with some of the idiots you've encountered over the years.

No, you've been amazing. You've resisted the temptation to have your car plastered with naff bumper stickers, or to have tinted windows, or a personalised number plate or spoilers or any of those other 'Look at me!' adornments. Ok, you may have had one or two of them, but that was when you were younger and more foolish. You probably used to wear daft clothes too, but we've all done it.

So, turn off the engine, sit back and recline your seat and settle down to the jokes, trivia, wit and wisdom enshrined in these pages. And try to ignore the beeping of all those horns behind you!

Mike Haskins and Clive Whichelow

OLD BANGERS

No other man-made device since the shields and lances of the ancient knights fulfils a man's ego like an automobile.

Sir William Rootes (chairman of Rootes Group, British automobile manufacturer)

The World's First Motor Car

One of the world's first motor cars was of course the Model T Ford. Or was it? Actually, the Model T Ford ran off the production line for the first time in 1908. The very first motor car – one with an internal combustion engine – was built 46 years before that by Belgian J.J. Etienne Lenoir. So, next time someone says there's never been a famous Belgian hit them with that!

So why aren't we all driving round in Lenoirs now, with the name of the pioneering J.J. on our lips whenever the motor car is mentioned? Well, Monsieur Lenoir had other ideas. After knocking out the world's first motor car (which actually looked more like a cross between a three-wheeled pram and a portable whelk stall), the industrious J.J. started working on the world's first motor boat. No slouch, he.

Incidentally, if you're ever asked in a pub quiz 'who ordered the very first motor car from J.J. Lenoir?' you will be able impress everyone by saying that it was Tsar Alexander II of Russia. Not a lot of people know that.

Oh, and before we allow the Belgians to run away with all the credit regarding combustion engines, let us not forget that according to Guinness World Records the very first practical combustion engine vehicle was built by (cue Land of Hope and Glory) Englishman Samuel Brown who whipped up Shooter's Hill, Kent, in May 1826, a full thirty-six years before young J.J. had got off the blocks.

———

What Englishman will give his mind to politics as long as he can afford to keep a motor car?

George Bernard Shaw

Driving in the 1670s

According to some sources the invention of the first car dates back not to the 19th century as is usually supposed but 200 years further to the late 17th century.

Ferdinand Verbiest was a Jesuit priest and astronomer born in what is now Belgium. He was sent to China in 1658 as part of an evangelical mission but at first this did not go well.

Verbiest sailed from Lisbon with a passenger list that included 36 other missionaries and the Viceroy of the Indies. When he arrived in Macau only 10 of the passengers had survived the voyage. The Jesuit missionaries subsequently suffered persecution in China for teaching false religion. They were eventually condemned to death by strangulation. This sentence was then judged to be too lenient and was amended to being cut into pieces while still alive.

Against the odds Verbiest won favour with the young Chinese Emperor and was appointed head of the imperial Bureau of Mathematics. In this capacity he went on to design a small steam driven car to amuse the Emperor and his court. The car is described in Latin in Verbiest's book *Astronomia Europae* and is believed to date to some time between 1679 and 1681.

Verbiest's car had steam from a boiler striking the blades of a

horizontal wheel which then meshed with the vehicle's front wheels. According to one account the truck turned around in the courtyard of the Imperial Palace to the great enthusiasm of the spectators.

However the machine was only 2 feet long and lacked any provision for a driver or passengers, and some historians are unconvinced it was ever built. This therefore makes it a bit of a stretch to claim Verbiest's invention as the world's first motor car.

I have found my drives to improve my general health. The jolting which occurs when a motor car is driven at fair speed conduces to healthy agitation that acts on the liver. This aids the peristaltic movements of the bowels and promotes the performance of their functions.

Dr William Thomson, Journal of Medicine, 1901 (he also advised running smartly for two to three hundred yards after a 20-mile drive to compensate for the difference in exercise derived from riding a horse)

The World's First Motor Car Trip

Although M. Lenoir invented his motor car in Paris in May 1862 it was not until September 1863 that he plucked up the courage to take it out on the road. What was he worried about? Whatever it was, it can't have been all the other traffic, because there wasn't any – apart of course from the horses, carts, donkeys, penny-farthings, and occasional escaped pig. Actually, perhaps that's why he waited sixteen months. He set off from the Societe de Moteurs Lenoir in the appropriately named Rue de la Roquette and drove six miles to Joinville-le-Pont. The entire return journey took three hours, averaging four miles an hour, so probably not much faster than a present-day commute through Paris then.

The World's First Gas Guzzler

The Lenoir car ran on liquid hydrocarbon fuel, but the first car to run on petrol was built by Frenchman Edouard Delamare-Deboutteville in 1883. Unfortunately the vehicle he used was not robust enough to cope with the throbbing power of the 8hp engine. He went on to work with stationary engines instead and ended up winning the Legion d'honneur for his troubles.

In the meantime Carl Benz had been working on his petrol engine in Germany and started rolling out a stream of petrol driven cars from 1885 onwards. The first had a mere three-quarters of a horse power engine, which would make a coach and four horses more than five times more powerful. Nevertheless it didn't stop the Benz company continuing to improve and perfect their motor cars until they were fit for their first public demonstration in July 1886. The half-mile trip in Mannheim amazed passers-by with speeds of up to 8 mph, though little did they realise that the drive was achieved by the use of bicycle chains. You can't knock old technology.

At Last... The Official Inventor Of The Motor Car!

According to Daimler-Benz (makers of Mercedes-Benz cars) the automobile was invented in 1886 by Karl Benz and Gottlieb Daimler. This claim is based on the definition of an automobile being a light carriage for personal transport with three or four wheels, powered by a liquid-fuelled internal combustion engine.

Gottlieb Daimler had however invented the gas powered motorcycle in 1885 which also fits the definition for an automobile.

Working just 60 miles away from Daimler's workshop, Karl Benz developed his Motorwagen in 1885. This was a three wheeled horseless carriage powered by a four-stroke engine which is clearly the direct ancestor of today's cars – particularly the Reliant Robin!

This 'automobile fuelled by gas' was patented on January 29, 1886 as patent number DRP-37435. So if that happens to be the registration number of your car, it could be worth something!

What a lucky thing the wheel was invented before the automobile; otherwise, can you imagine what awful screeching?

Samuel Hoffenstein

The First Time A Car Was Borrowed By The Wife And Kids

Although Benz is generally recognised as the inventor of the petrol powered automobile, he at first had difficulty in persuading the public to buy his new invention. And then on the August 5, 1888, Benz's wife, Bertha, and their two sons, Eugen (15) and Richard (13), decided to borrow dad's car without his knowledge.

With the two boys operating the tiller, mum and the kids drove the car from Benz's workshop in Mannheim to visit Bertha's mother in Pforzheim, 100 km away. They had to buy benzin from apothecary shops along the way to keep the engine running as well as leather from a cobbler to fix the brakes. They pushed the car up any steep hills and eventually arrived in Pforzheim late that evening.

They sent a telegram to Carl to say where they had got to before returning the following day. The trip had however garnered much attention along the route. So perhaps Bertha hadn't just been intending to her mother after all but had instead staged a massive publicity stunt that finally kick-started public interest in her husband's business.

Also on her return Bertha was able to suggest many improvements to the car including the addition of a low gear so you didn't have to get out and push it up the hills!

What I like, or one of the things I like, about motoring is the sense it gives one of lighting accidentally, like a voyager who touches another planet with the tip of his toe, upon scenes which would have gone on, have always gone on, will go on, unrecorded, save for this chance glimpse. Then it seems to me I am allowed to see the heart of the world uncovered for a moment.

Virginia Woolf

Mr Koosen's New Car

In November 1895, Mr J.A. Koosen of Portsmouth purchased a 5-horsepower Lutzmann car. Mr Koosen was disappointed however to find his new car would not start. After two days of frustration, the source of the problem was discovered. Mr Koosen was informed that in order for the car to go, you first had to put some petrol into it. And he can't have been the only driver in those early days to be so naïve.

After this, Mr Koosen's car seemed to run a little more smoothly although the vehicle clearly remained quite a novelty in the locality. Mr Koosen's wife recorded in her diary for December 9, 1895:

'Drove to Lee at 10; motor sparked at once and went well. After lunch started for home in motor car; came round by Fareham; had lovely drive; police spotted us; awful crowd followed us at Cosham; had to beat them off with an umbrella.'

The civilized man has built a coach, but has lost the use of his feet.

Ralph Waldo Emerson

Burning Some Rubber

In 1845 Scottish engineer R.W. Thompson patented the world's first pneumatic tyre. Thompson's invention comprised a heavy rubber outer layer stretched around metal rims and an inflatable tube. Unfortunately no-one was very interested in this in 1845! In 1888 John Boyd Dunlop also patented a pneumatic rubber tyre. Two years later the patent was revoked when someone discovered Thompson had already invented the same thing 43 years earlier.

In 1891 Édouard and André Michelin were granted a patent for a removable pneumatic tyre. Really they should have thought of this earlier as at least one of them had a body that was clearly made up entirely of tyres. Or at least that's the way he always looks when depicted in the company's marketing material!

A Drive To Berwick

'Towards the end of February, 1896 I started out at 10.30pm for Berwick, a distance of 30 miles.

'Arriving at Berwick at 3am, I proceeded to picnic under the shadow of the town hall and was there soon surrounded by the entire police force on duty, 13 men in all.

'I was eventually fined the large sum of 6d with 19s 6d costs for using a horseless carriage without having a man on foot preceding it.'

T.R.B. Eliot,
driver of an 1895 Paris-built 3.5hp Panhard Phaeton

Two Gallons Of Unleaded Launch Spirit, Please!

In 1893 Frederick Richard Simms suggested 'petrol' as a name for a substance he wished to buy from Carless, Capel & Leonard of Hackney Wick. Carless, Capel & Leonard was a British chemical company that distilled heavy oil for heating and lighting. The light fuel that left over from this process was regarded as a waste product and sold off as cleaning fluid.

Simms had purchased the rights for the use of Daimler's internal combustion engine in the UK. He established what may have been the first British motor company in 1893. In that year Simms ordered 100 gallons a month of Carless' cleaning fluid which became known as 'launch spirit'.

Simms suggested that the name 'petrol' should be used for the substance. This was very similar to 'petroleum' which was at the time the trade name for paraffin oil. Nevertheless 'petrol' was registered as a trademark by Carless, Capel & Leonard and until the 1930s their competitors had to use the term 'motor spirit' to describe the same substance. Petrol subsequently became the generic term.

In the USA, the term gasoline became the generally used name. The term 'gasolene' was coined in 1865 and the current spelling appeared in 1871. It was never registered as a trade name although it is similar to other petroleum products of the late 19th century. The petroleum jelly Vaseline was, for example, patented in 1872. The name kerosene had been coined in 1846 by the Canadian geologist Abraham Gesner for a fluid distilled from coal.

Sign seen in US desert: Last chance to buy fuel. Next five petrol stations are mirages.

All of the biggest technological inventions created by man – the airplane, the automobile, the computer – say little about his intelligence, but speak volumes about his laziness.

Mark Kennedy

Average Petrol Prices
In The UK Through The Ages

Prices are per gallon

1896   9d (that's 3.75 new pence per gallon and at this stage there was no tax on petrol!)

1909   13½d (including tax which has been introduced at 3d per gallon)

1914   20d

1918   43 ½d (tax is now 13.79% having leapt up to 24% in 1915)

1928   14 ½d (between 1920 and 1928 there was no tax again!)

1939   20.37d (tax is back and is now 44.2%)

1945   24d (that's 2 shillings or 10 new pence)

1956   64d (a price peak around the time of the Suez Crisis)

1960   55.83d (tax is now 53.73%)

1970   80d (that's 6 shillings 8d or about 33.3 new pence – tax is 67.5%)

1974   49.6p (following decimalisation we're into new pence)

1975   73.2p

1980   128.5p (more than £1 per gallon for the first time!)

1985   199.8p (tax is now 54%)

1990   213.5p (but now you can get unleaded for just 194.4p per gallon)

1995   273.4p (tax is 75.41% – unleaded is 246.38p per gallon)

2000   389p (367.19p per gallon for unleaded)

2005   396.53p per gallon of unleaded including 68.89% tax

The Ford Quadricycle

Henry Ford was born near Detroit, Michigan on 30th July 1863. He was the son of William Ford, a farmer from County Cork and Mary Litogot Ford, the daughter of Belgian immigrants.

As a teenager Henry became expert at dismantling and re-assembling watches. In his twenties he developed an expertise in operating the family farm's steam engine. At the age of 28 he got a job with Thomas Edison's company, The Edison Illuminating Company and by 1893 he was their chief engineer.

Two years later Ford got his friends Jim Bishop, George Cato, Edward (Spider) Huff, and David Bell, to help him build create his first gasoline powered car: the Quadricycle!

And it was quite literally a quadricycle with its chassis being supported by four bicycle wheels. The machine was powered by a two cylinder engine which Ford had based on a design he had found in the January 1896 edition of American Machinist magazine. First gear took you along at 10 mph, second gear at 20 mph. There was no reverse gear.

When the vehicle was finished, Ford discovered he had shown a slight lack of foresight in his design. The Quadricycle was too wide to go out of the door of the workshop in which Ford had built it. Instead Ford used an axe to make an impromptu adjustment to the door space.

He then set off for his first spin round the block at 4 am on June 4, 1896. A few blocks later the Quadricycle stalled and refused to start again. Lacking breakdown cover, Ford was forced to sit there for a while suffering abuse from passers by.

Nevertheless it was effectively the beginning of the Ford empire. Ford was encouraged in his endeavours by his employer, Thomas Edison, who, on hearing about the vehicle, told him, 'That's the thing! Keep at it!'

LEGAL CONCERNS

That the automobile has practically reached the limit of its development is suggested by the fact that during the past year no improvements of a radical nature have been introduced.

Scientific American (June 2, 1909)

Weird US Driving Laws

In Alabama it has been officially declared illegal to drive while wearing a blindfold.

Alaska has outlawed the practice of driving with a dog tethered to the roof of the vehicle.

In Arkansas it is illegal to sound your horn in any area where cold beverages or sandwiches are served after 9 p.m.

It is against the law in California to jump from a car travelling at 65 mph or for a woman to drive while wearing a housecoat. It is also illegal for a vehicle without a driver to exceed to 60 mph.

In Sarasota, Florida the fine for hitting a pedestrian is a very reasonable $78 a time.

In Florida, if an elephant, goat or alligator is left tied to a parking meter, the parking fee has to be paid just as it would for a vehicle.

In Dublin, Georgia you are officially prohibited from driving your vehicle through children's playgrounds.

In Evanston, Illinois it is illegal to change clothes in an automobile with the curtains drawn, except in case of fire.

In Kansas it is against the law to transport dead poultry on Kansas Avenue, Topeka. So, as many have noted, you should avoid this route on your way home from KFC.

In Derby, Kansas screeching your tyres will earn you a 30 day jail sentence

Swearing from a vehicle is a misdemeanour in Rockville, Maryland.

It's illegal for your vehicle to leave dirt or sticky substances on any road in Minnetonka, Minnesota.

In University City, Missouri it is illegal to sound the horn of someone else's vehicle.

In Montana, it is illegal to have a sheep in the cab of your truck without a chaperone.

It is against the law to place a bench or chair in the middle of the road in Reno, Nevada.

In Blairstown, New Jersey it is forbidden to plant trees in the middle of the road.

In Sag Harbor, New York it is also illegal TO disrobe while in your vehicle.

In Dunn, North Carolina it is illegal to play in traffic, it is illegal to drive through a cemetery if you're not there to bury someone and it is illegal to drive on the sidewalk.

It is against the law to run out of fuel in Youngstown, Ohio.

In Oregon you must yield to pedestrians when driving on the sidewalk, it is an offence to leave your car door open longer than is deemed necessary and it is a Class A traffic violation to use your car on a highway to demonstrate your physical endurance.

In Pennsylvania any motorist driving along a country road at night must stop every mile and send up a rocket signal. He must then wait ten minutes for the road to be cleared of livestock before continuing.

Also in Pennsylvania any motorist who sights a team of horses coming toward him must pull well off the road, cover his car with a blanket or canvas that blends with the countryside, and let the horses pass.

In Tennessee, it is illegal TO shoot any game other than whales from a moving automobile.

Turn For The Worse

A man is taking his son to school, when by mistake he makes an illegal turn at a junction lights. 'Oh no!' the man says cursing. 'I just made an illegal turn!' 'No need to worry, Dad,' replies his son. 'There's a police car behind us and it just did exactly the same thing!'

The Highway Code (Then And Now)

The first edition of *The Highway Code* was published in the UK in 1931. This means that some people had been driving for almost 30 years without bothering with any rules. Nothing's changed then. Except, of course, that people now are at least expected to read the *Highway Code*, and, of course, to be tested on it before being allowed on the road.

In 1931 the *Highway Code* cost one penny, today it's £2.50. Though, to be fair, it is a lot longer. The 1931 edition had just 18 pages, the current version has 152.

By the time the second edition of the *Highway Code* came out it showed pictures of traffic signs. Ten of them. That's right, ten! These days you can encounter at least as many as that just for various animals that might be crossing the road ahead: snakes, frogs, toads, elephants, tortoises, you name it.

In fact, there's now an entire book you can buy as a sort of companion volume to the *Highway Code* that features nothing but road signs. At 144 pages, *Know Your Traffic Signs* is almost as long as the *Highway Code* itself, and at £4.99 double the price. Enjoy!

New Driving Licence

A woman gets her new driving licence and complains to her husband that her picture on it makes her look really grumpy. 'That's all right,' says her husband. 'When you get pulled over by the police, it'll exactly match how you look.'

You May Tax Your Steam Powered Vehicle Here

The 1861 Locomotive Act introduced taxation of all steam-powered vehicles. In 1903 the Motor Car Act set an annual registration of £1 for cars – that's the equivalent of about £74 today – requiring all vehicles to be registered and to display registration marks in a prominent position.

The first registration marks consisted of one letter and one number. The first registration, A1, was issued by London County Council.

The displayable tax disc was introduced in 1919.

Driving licences were introduced in 1901. You could get one for a fee of five shillings (25p) from Post Office. These first licences were however solely for identification purpose.

Parking Meters

The coin-operated meter was invented by American lawyer Carlton Cole 'Carl' Magee who took out patent number 2118318 on May 13, 1935. His patent application begins:

'My invention relates to meters for measuring the time of occupancy or use of parking or other space, for the use of which it is desirous an incidental charge be made upon a time basis.'

The authorities thought that this was such a good idea that the world's first parking meter was installed in the business district of Oklahoma City on July 19, 1935 – just two months after Magee's patent!

Today there are estimated to be 5 million meters in the USA. If each of these meters takes just $1 a day from Monday to Saturday, the income would add up to over $1.5 billion dollars a year. And in reality they probably take a great deal more money than that!

London got its first parking meter in Grosvenor Square in 1958. Six hundred and twenty five meters were initially installed in London with a charge of 6d (2½p) an hour to park. If your meter was found to have expired you would however have been landed with a fixed penalty of £2, which is equivalent to £100 today.

On the other hand, the Bible contains much that is relevant today, like Noah taking 40 days to find a place to park.

Curtis McDougall

A real patriot is the fellow who gets a parking ticket and rejoices that the system works.

Bill Vaughan

I solved the parking problem – I bought a parked car!

Anon

Yesterday I parked my car in a tow-away zone. When I came back the entire area was gone.

Steven Wright

Traffic Wardens

When the Beatles released their ode to a traffic warden or 'meter maid' Lovely Rita in 1967 we had only seen these parking police on our streets for seven years. Feels like they've been around forever now, doesn't it?

Ticket Off!

A driver pulls up by a traffic warden. 'If I park on these double yellow lines and pop over the road to the newsagent will you give me a ticket?' asks the driver. 'Yes I will,' replies the warden. 'But,' says the driver, 'all the other cars here are parked on the double yellow lines already.' 'I know,' replies the warden. 'But none of them asked me to give them a ticket.'

The Human Ticket Machine

In 2009 traffic warden Geoffrey Stobbart appeared in national newspapers for setting a record for the number of parking tickets dished out. In his first two months in the job, The Human Ticket Machine as he became known, handed out 416 of the yellow things. Imagine what he'll be like with a bit more practice! The previous record holder was John Woodgate, known as The Terminator, who handed out 11,000 tickets in eleven years in Haverhill, Suffolk.

Bog Standard Parking

In 2008 a man was so annoyed at getting a parking ticket he wrote the cheque for the fine on two sheets of toilet paper. The court in Long Melford, Suffolk accepted the cheque but demanded that he pay a further £15 to cover the cost of cashing it. He refused and was taken to court for non-payment of the fine. In the end the judge let him off but made him sit at the back of the court for the day as a punishment!

Serving In The Parking Front Line

In 2000 the BBC reported that over thirty police forces in Great Britain had issued traffic wardens with stab-proof and bullet-proof vests to help protect them from irate motorists.

When I get real bored, I like to drive down town and get a great parking spot, then sit in my car and count how many people ask me if I'm leaving.

Steven Wright

Some Cow Gave
Me a Parking Ticket!

Way back in 1963, in the early days of the joys of traffic wardens, a Sussex farmer wired his car up with a device normally used for keeping cattle in their place. He claimed that it was mainly intended to stop people from stealing his car but conceded that it would also be handy for keeping wardens away from slapping parking tickets on it. He reckoned that his device was capable of giving out quite a shock. Two thousand volts to be precise!

Have you ever wondered why, when a car has been left somewhere so it's causing an obstruction, they think the best thing to do is to clamp it so it can't be driven away?

Anon

The Top 10 Illegal Things
UK Drivers Admit To Doing

1. Breaking the speed limit

2. Using a handheld mobile phone whilst driving

3. Overtaking another car in a dangerous manner

4. Pressing the horn to get others to speed up and move out of the way

5. Jumping or running a red light

6. Driving the wrong way on a one way street

7. Parking illegally

8. Parking in space reserved either for disabled drivers or for parents with small children

9. Eating and drinking while driving

10. Changing clothing while driving

I drive with my knees. Otherwise how can I put on my lipstick and talk on the phone?

Sharon Stone

Legal Or Not?

In the UK activities such as eating, smoking, applying make-up, map reading and tuning the radio are not against the law as such.

Nevertheless if you do any of these things you can be charged with careless driving or failing to be in proper control of your vehicle.

One time a cop pulled me over for running a stop sign. He said, 'Didn't you see the stop sign?' I said, 'Yeah, but I don't believe everything I read.'

Steven Wright

Are You Taking The Pee?

A policeman stops a driver who has been driving erratically and asks him to blow into a breathalyser. 'I can't do that,' says the man. 'I suffer from asthma and I'm terribly short of breath.' 'OK,' says the policeman. 'Then we'll have to take a urine sample.' 'Sorry,' says the man. 'I went just five minutes ago.' 'All right then,' says the policeman. 'It'll have to be a blood sample.' 'I can't do that either,' replies the man. 'I'm a haemophiliac.' 'Right,' says the policeman, beginning to get slightly annoyed. 'I want you to walk in a straight line along the yellow line at the side of the road.' 'Oh, I can't do that, officer,' says the man. 'I'm far too drunk.'

If you get a ticket, you can go to traffic school, and they make you watch movies for like eight hours: head-on collisions, mannequins flying out the windshield. At the end of the movie, the instructor goes, 'Now what have we learned by this?' Never let a mannequin drive your car!

Robert Schimmel

Going Against The Flow

A policeman stops a woman who has been driving the wrong way up a one way street. 'Where do you think you're going?' he asks. 'I don't know,' says the woman, 'but I think I must be late. Everyone else is coming back!'

Driving Laws From Around The World

In the Catholic states of southern Germany it is illegal to wash your car on a Sunday.

In Germany, drivers must stop at a pedestrian crossing if there is a pedestrian waiting to cross.

Finland's Supreme Court has ruled taxi drivers must pay 22 Euros a year in royalty fees for playing music in their cabs. If they have a customer in the back seat this of course constitutes a public musical performance!

In Australia taxi drivers can be penalised if they do not have an armload of hay in their vehicles. In fact this law can be found in section 51 of the London Hackney Carriage Act 1831 when a coachman would have been the equivalent of a taxi driver and thus had to carry hay to feed his horses. The law was not amended in Britain until 1976 and it is believed that it has not so far been repealed in Australia.

It is illegal to drive in Manila between 7:00 am and 7:00 pm on Monday if your number plate ends in a number 1 or 2. That might actually be quite sensible because it's designed to help reduce traffic congestion. Number plates ending in 3 and 4 are banned on Tuesdays and so on...

For every 'Drive Safely' sign, shouldn't there be a 'Resume Normal Driving' sign?

Robert Brault

THE NEED FOR SPEED

Speed has never killed anyone. Suddenly becoming stationary...
that's what gets you.

Jeremy Clarkson

Special Licence

Harry is driving down the centre of the road at 100 mph. A
policeman pulls him over. 'Let's see your licence,' says the
policeman. 'I know what you're going to say,' says Harry, 'but
don't worry! I have a special licence that allows me to drive like
this.' 'Rubbish!' says the policeman. 'I've never heard of such
a thing.' 'Well, just have a look at this!' says Harry pulling his
licence out of his pocket. 'But that's just an ordinary driving
licence,' says the officer. 'No! Look at the bottom!' says Harry.
'See where it says, "Tear along the dotted line"!'

Excuses Given To Police
By Drivers Caught Speeding

I had passed out after seeing flashing lights, which I believed to be
UFOs in the distance. The flash of the camera brought me round
from my trance.

I was in the airport's flight path and I believe the camera was
triggered by a jet overhead, not my car.

There was a strong wind behind my car which pushed me over
the limit.

My friend had just chopped his fingers off and I was rushing
the fingers to hospital.

The vibrations from the surfboard I had on the roof rack set
off the camera.

I had to rush my dying hamster to the vet's.

31

Built For Speed

The first maximum speed limit in the world was imposed in Great Britain under the Locomotives on Highways Act of 1861. The maximum speed allowed by the act was 10 mph and 5 mph in towns. That's rather slower than a horse could have travelled and with the potential for just as much damage, particularly if you happened to be pulling a cartful of manure behind you.

Amazingly, this already modest speed limit was lowered by the Locomotive Act of 1865 to just 4 mph and that was just for country roads. In towns the speed limit became a piffling 2 mph. It would have literally been quicker to walk. And it was also under the 1865 act that the famous 'man with a red flag' came into the picture. A man with a red flag (or lantern, if at night time) had to walk in front of what would then have been steam powered traction engines warning pedestrians and other road users that a vehicle was bringing up the rear at the highly dangerous speed of 2 mph (or 4 mph if it was in the country). When the first cars began to appear, their drivers hoped that they would be classed as horse-less carriages and thus exempt from the provisions of the 1865 act. Unfortunately for the country's first drivers, it was decided that their cars were 'road locomotives' and that they were covered by the terms of the act!

It wasn't until 1896 that the law was changed again. Motor cars were now placed under the category of light locomotives and the speed limit was increased to a mind-blowing 14 mph. In celebration of this earth-shattering change in the law, the famous London to Brighton car rally was inaugurated in the same year.

I've Been Waiting For You

A policeman climbs out of his car and strides over to have a word with a boy he's just stopped for speeding. 'I've been sitting here waiting for you all day,' says the policeman. 'Have you?' says the boy. 'Well, I got here as fast as I could.'

How Many Horses?

The term horsepower was invented by James Watt, the inventor of the steam engine. The concept emerged not from horses pulling carriages but from ponies used to haul coal from a mine. Watt's basic notion was that one horse was capable of lifting 330 pounds of coal by 100 feet in a minute although in reality this was quite an optimistic expectation. By comparison one horsepower is the equivalent of 745.699 watts or .746 kilowatts and a healthy human being can sustain about 0.1 horsepower.

Between 1922 and 1947 a formula devised by the RAC was used for calculating motor tax on cars based on their horsepower. The formula was $D^2N/2.5$, in which D was the diameter or bore of the cylinder measured in inches, N the number of cylinders and 2.5 a constant. This was however a rather dubious method which gave very low assessments of horsepower.

25 mph In The Outside Lane

A car is driving at 25 mph on the outside lane of a motorway causing traffic to back for miles behind. The police manage to intercept the car and find a sweet little old lady at the wheel. In the passenger seat is another old lady as white as a sheet and sitting bolt upright with a look of horror frozen on her face. The police ask the old lady driver if she knew what speed she had been doing. 'There isn't a problem is there, officer?' she asks. 'I always drive at the speed it says on the sign.' 'And what speed was that?' asks the policeman. 'Well, just now I saw a sign saying A30, so I drove at 30 miles per hour. Then we turned onto the motorway and saw a sign saying M25 so I slowed down to 25 miles per hour. Isn't that correct?' The policeman notices that the old lady's passenger hasn't moved a muscle since they started talking and starts to worry she may have died. 'Is your friend alright?' asks the policeman. 'I'm not sure,' says the old lady driver. 'She's been like this ever since we were on the A150.'

The World's Fastest Production Cars

Any list of the world's fastest cars is going to be subject to claim and counter claim and nit-picking about over what distance the speed was achieved and all the rest of it. And depending on where you get your information you may find that the speed claimed for each car is slightly different every time. But frankly, whether your car can go at 243 or 245 mph may not be the first thing on your mind as you grip the steering wheel for dear life, the colour drains from your knuckles and your face and you find yourself mouthing a silent prayer....

So, here are what seem to be generally agreed to be the world's fastest production cars and their approximate top speeds (their place in the list may vary because of the differences in reported speeds):

SSC Ultimate Aero: around 256–257 mph

Bugatti Veyron: around 252–253 mph

Saleen S7 Twin-Turbo: around 248 mph

Koenigsegg CCX: around 245–252 mph

McLaren F1: around 240 mph.

Ferrari Enzo: around 217 mph

Jaguar XJ220: around 217 mph

Pagani Zonda F: around 215 mph

Lamborghini Murcielago LP640: around 211–213 mph

Porsche Carrera GT: around 205–209 mph

100 Years Ago We Could All Have Been Record Holders!

The world's first ever land speed record for a car was set on December 18, 1898 between the villages of St. Germain and Constans near Paris.

The car was built by the manufacturer Jeantaud for the Marquis de Chasseloup-Laubat, a founder member of the Automobile Club de France. The Marquis could presumably have gone down in history for having set the record himself but being an aristocrat he took a chauffeur with him in the form of his younger brother, Count Gaston ('The Electric Count').

Together the pair managed to get up to the extraordinary speed of 39.245 mph. Their car was not a petrol driven vehicle however. Instead the Jeantaud was powered by an electric motor and alkaline batteries. It is also believed that it was the first car to use a modern steering wheel rather than a tiller.

Of course in the very early days of motoring it was presumably possible to set a world land speed record every time you left your house. And indeed just under one month after the de Chasseloup-Laubat brothers' triumph, their record was smashed. On January 17, 1899, Belgian driver Camille Jenatzy ('Le Diable Rouge' or 'The Red Devil') reached 41.42 mph again in an electric car. This record lasted even less time than the first. Count Gaston immediately seized the record back the same day by reaching 43.69 mph.

This must have particularly irked Camille Jenatzy, on the event of whose death in 1913, the *New York Times* recorded, 'As an illustration of his irascible temperament, it is related that during one race he jumped from his car and struck an inoffensive onlooker whose demeanour displeased him.'

The land speed record alternated between the Red Devil and the Electric Count over the next few weeks of 1899. By April 29,

Jenatzy was up to 65.79 mph and this record stood for three years. Jenatzy predicted he would die in a Mercedes. His prediction proved to be accurate although possibly not in the way he had envisaged. In 1913 Jenatzy went out hunting with some friends. By way of an amusing prank he hid behind a bush and tricked his companions by making a noise like a wild animal. His friends immediately shot him, wounding him in the thigh. Jenatzy then bled to death while his friends attempted to get him to hospital in their car which was, as predicted, a Mercedes.

Your Personal Speed Limit

The way to calculate what your personal speed limit on the motorway should be: subtract your age from 100. Double this number if your car has dual exhaust. Conversely, add your age to 100 if you are suffering a midlife crisis!

The other day I got pulled over for speeding. The officer said, 'Don't you know the speed limit is only 55 miles an hour?' I said, 'Yeah, I know, but I'm not going to be out that long.'

Steven Wright

Speeding Around The World

Today the speed limit on most UK motorways is 70 mph (113kph). By contrast, the country with one of the lowest speed limits is Macau with motorway limits of between 37-49 mph (60-80 kph)

The highest speed limit in the world may currently be on Polish motorways where you can get up to around 87 mph (140kph) without getting a ticket.

In 2006 Austria tried out a variable 160 kph (99 mph) limit on motorways.

In Germany over 50% of the autobahn system has no speed limit. The autobahn does however have an advisory speed limit of 80 mph (130 kph).

Before 1974 and between 1995 and 1999, the speed limit on most rural roads in the US State Montana was expressed in a non numerical manner as 'reasonable and prudent'. Presumably the police were equipped with speed guns specially adapted to identify vehicles engaged in acts of imprudence.

But if you really want to put your foot down, neither the motorways in Peru nor Venezuela have any speed limit at all.

There is however only one country in the world which has no speed limit whatsoever: the Isle of Man. The Isle of Man is also quite a small country so if you do get up to a particularly impressive speed there is a genuine danger that you will accidentally shoot off the end into the Irish Sea.

OK. The Isle of Man does have speed restrictions in certain areas but there is no national speed limit although there was a recent attempt to introduce one. This was however decisively rejected by the public. Of 408 letters submitted during a public consultation on the matter, 281 (69%) were firmly against the idea of introducing a speed limit.

It is interesting to note that of the 281 people who took the trouble to write opposing the introduction of a speed limit on the Isle of Man, 42 were not from the island at all!

Hooking Another One In

A man is speeding along a dual carriageway when a policeman pulls him over.

'But it's not fair,' says the driver. 'There were loads of other cars doing the same speed as me – why didn't you stop them as well?'

'Have you ever done any fishing?' asks the policeman.

'Yeah...' says the man hesitantly, wondering why he asked.

'Did you ever catch *all* the fish?'

Excuses Given To Police By Drivers Caught Speeding

A violent sneeze caused a chain reaction where my foot pushed down harder on the accelerator.

There was a suspected case of foot and mouth and I had to rush to see the cow concerned.

The only way I could demonstrate my faulty clutch was to accelerate madly.

I was going downhill.

I have oversized tyres.

I was passing a truck.

My car can't go that fast. (An excuse once attempted by the driver of a BMW 540)

I was just keeping up with traffic.

Do You Know What Speed You Were Just Doing, Sir?

According to the TV series *Top Gear*, Arthur Chirkinian holds the record for the fastest ever speeding ticket in the United States. Chirkinian was alleged to have broken the speed limit in a 75 mph (121 kph) zone in west Texas in May 2003. And 'breaking the speed limit' is putting it mildly. Arthur Chirkinian was alleged to have been travelling at 242 mph (389 kph) at the time. This would therefore mean that he had been exceeding the speed limit by an impressive 220%.

Chirkinian had been competing in the San Francisco to Miami Gumball 3000 Rally. His car was a Koenigsegg CCR. The basic price for the car is said to be $590,000 and 242 mph would theoretically be possible as this is the vehicle's stated top speed.

There is also an additional twist to the story. After his arrest, Chirkinian retrieved his car from the police pound. When he attempted to catch up with his competitors in the rally, he discovered that the car's radiator cap had disappeared. The manufacturers informed Chirkinian that the only other generally available radiator cap that would fit the car was that for the VW Beetle. According to the story, Chirkinian went to the nearest VW dealership, purchased a brand new Turbo Beetle, drove it back to his Koenigsegg CCR, took the radiator cap from the Beetle, fitted it in the Koenigsegg and drove off to re-join the race leaving a brand new VW Beetle behind at the side of the road with the keys in the ignition.

In *Gumball 3000: The Movie*, Arthur Chirkinian does indeed say, 'You don't buy a new car just for the radiator cap every day!'

Give Me One Good Excuse

A man is speeding along the motorway in a brand-new Ferrari. He hits 90 mph and then puts his foot down a little further till the speed is edging up to 100 mph. He then hears a siren and looks in his mirror to see a police car chasing him.

'Hah!' thinks the man. 'There's no way that they are going to catch a Ferrari!'

He speeds up to 110 mph, and then 120 mph. But still the police car is on his tail. Even when he gets up to 135 mph the police car manages to get alongside him and signals for him to pull over.

The man does so and the policeman says, 'Look, mate, it's Friday night, I'm just about to go off duty for a long weekend, I've already got a stack of paperwork back at the station, and frankly I don't need any more, so if you can give me one good reason why you were speeding, go ahead, and I might just let you off.'

'Well, officer,' says the man. 'A couple of weeks ago my wife ran off with a policeman and I thought you were coming to give her back.'

'Have a good weekend,' says the officer.

The World's First Speeding Ticket

The world's first ever speeding ticket is said to have been given in Dayton, Ohio in 1904.

According to Ohio History Central:

'Throughout most of the twentieth century, the city of Detroit, Michigan, was synonymous with American automobile manufacturing. In the late nineteenth and early twentieth centuries, that was not the case. Instead, Ohio innovators in Cleveland and elsewhere were at the forefront of this new form of transportation technology.

'Because of Ohio's important role in the early automobile industry, the state was the site of numerous firsts in automobile history. Among these firsts was the first speeding ticket for an automobile driver.'

So in other words, the good people of Ohio built the cars and then invented the idea of handing out speeding tickets to the people who were driving away having just bought them.

The recipient of the world's first speeding ticket was Harry Myers. Myers had been caught travelling at 12 mph on West Third Street.

Harry Myers was a star of early Hollywood films. He appeared in 245 films and worked with the likes of Charlie Chaplin, Buster Keaton and Mary Pickford before his death in 1938.

This surely explains why he has gone down in history as Hollywood's first jetsetting, bad boy, 12 mph speed freak!

However, in their haste to claim the world's first speeding ticket, the Americans seemed to have overlooked the fact that on January 28, 1899 a speeding ticket was issued in Britain to Mr Walter Arnold who was fined one shilling (5p). Mr Arnold had been caught travelling at 8 mph in a 2 mph area. Yes! We British were racing along and breaking the speed limit years before the Yanks!

And at 8 mph could it have theoretically been possible for the police to have caught Mr Arnold's speeding vehicle just by walking at an especially brisk pace before leaning into the car to glance at the speedometer?

Keep The Change!

American boxer Jack Johnson, the Galveston Giant, (1878–1948) was famously once pulled over for speeding. The officer who had stopped him gave Johnson a ticket for the then huge amount of $50. Johnson handed over a $100 bill to pay the fine. Johnson told him he could keep the change because he intended to drive at the same speed when he was on his way back.

Speed Cameras

The number of speed cameras in use on Britain's roads is somewhere between 5,500 and 6,000. It's slightly worrying that no one seems to know exactly how many there are, though if you asked the average motorist he or she would probably guess that the figure was far higher. It has however been reported that the number of car crashes caused by speeding vehicles is just 5% of the total, which raises the question of what are all these cameras for?

In 2006 police statistics showed that six times as many car accidents were caused by drivers not paying attention to the road as by speeding. It wasn't recorded how many of those drivers not paying attention were distracted by speed cameras, real or imagined.

406 mph Through Cheshire

In January 2004 sales manager Peter O'Flynn was caught by a speed camera in Runcorn, Cheshire.

He received a speeding ticket through the post telling him he had been exceeding the speed limit by some degree. According to the camera he had been travelling at a speed of 406 mph. If that was the case he must have been in a terrible hurry to get away from Runcorn at the time.

Mr O'Flynn did not however agree that he had been travelling through the town centre at half the speed of sound. He told the press, 'I rarely speed and it's safe to say I'll contest this.'

When photographed by the speed camera, Mr O'Flynn had however been driving a Peugeot 406. Could the device therefore have been a very simplistic one that somehow confused the name of the car with the speed it was doing? In which case presumably his fine would have been ever worse if he had been in a Fiat 500, let alone a Peugeot 5008.

Ooh What A Giveaway!

A policeman pulls a car over in the high street and tells the driver that he had just been doing 80 mph in a 30 mph zone.

'I was only doing 30!' protests the driver.

Not according to my speed gun,' says the policeman

'I was only doing 30!' shouts the man indignantly

'Oh no you weren't!' says the policeman firmly. 'You were doing 80.'

'Look mate,' says the driver, 'I'm really starting to get annoyed now....'

But just then, the driver's wife leans across to his window and says, 'Constable, I think I should warn you about something.'

'What's that?' asks the policeman.

'You should never argue with my husband when he's been drinking.'

And Off You Pope...

The Pope goes on a visit to the USA. He is being driven around in an enormous limo when he tells his driver that he has always wanted to drive this sort of car. 'Well, why not have a go, your holiness,' says the driver. And so the Pope climbs into the driving seat, while the driver hops in the back off and they shoot at 80 mph. A few minutes later they are pulled over by the police. The traffic cop radios into the police station to tell them, 'We've got a VIP situation here. I just pulled someone over and they must be really, really important.' 'Who is it?' asks the station controller. 'I don't know,' says the traffic cop. 'But whoever he is, he's got the Pope as his driver!'

Excuses Given By Drivers Caught Speeding

My ex-girlfriend still has keys to my car and keeps taking it without asking. I didn't report this to the police.

I was in a hire car and the speedometer was in a different position. I was actually looking at the rev counter by mistake.

I picked up a hitchhiker who commented that they liked my car so I let this person drive the vehicle. I don't have their name or address.

My car was stolen overnight and returned to the same point. I didn't report this to the police, as the first thing I knew of the matter was when a notice of intended prosecution for speeding came through my door.

I was trying to sell my car and the person who was clocked by a speed camera was test driving the vehicle. (In fact the car turned out to be 50 miles away from the registered owner's home at the time of the offence – so that's quite a test drive!).

The World's Most
Expensive Speeding Ticket

What was reported at the time as the world's most expensive
speeding ticket was given to a motorcyclist in Finland in 2002.
Anssi Vanjoki had been caught driving his Harley Davidson at
75 kph (47 mph) in a 50kph (31 mph) zone in Helsinki.
In January 2002 he was given a fine of 116,000 euros (at the time
around £78,800).

The reason the fine was so great was that under Finnish
law, traffic fines are calculated to be in proportion to the latest
available data on the offender's income. And Mr Vanjoki
happened to be a director of Finnish telecommunications giant
Nokia.

In 1999, Mr Vanjoki had earned 14 million euros. His speeding
ticket was therefore worked out to be equivalent to 14 days pay.
Mr Vanjoki went on to successfully appeal against the amount,
claiming that his wages had gone down slightly since 1999. The
fine was duly reduced by 95%.

Previously in Finland, Internet millionaire Jaakko Rytsola had
paid a 35,000 euro fine in 2000. Then in 2004 Jussi Salonoja,
heir to a leading Finnish sausage business, was caught driving at
80 kph in a 40 kph zone. Mr Salonoja's earnings in 2002 were
around 7 million euros (4.7 million pounds). He was duly handed
a speeding ticket for 170,000 euros (£116,000).

Fighting A Speeding Ticket

A motorist from Bristol was so incensed to receive a speeding ticket that he went to enormous effort and expense to prove the speed camera that caught him was faulty.

Twenty one-year-old driver Dale Lyle received a ticket for driving his Honda Civic at 98 mph. He knew immediately that this could not be the case. His car was rubbish and it was clearly incapable of doing that kind of speed.

Dale tried putting this argument to the local magistrates who in response asked him to officially prove the crap-ness of his vehicle. The first problem in doing this was the fact that Dale had by now sold the car to a friend for £600. There was nothing for it. He had to take out a bank overdraft and buy the vehicle back.

Dale then had to pay an independent expert £600 to speed test the car at a driving circuit. Sure enough the vehicle proved only capable of achieving 85.4 mph in fourth gear and 81.3 mph in, what now seemed ironically entitled, fifth gear.

Dale next went to the trouble of obtaining the speed camera footage of the alleged offence. This turned out to show three other cars in the frame at the same time. Clearly it must have been one of the other vehicles that had been doing 98 mph as Dale's car evidently wasn't up to the job.

Dale thus successfully managed to get his £1,000 fine and six month ban overturned and it had only cost him £1,200. Unfortunately this also presumably meant that Dale was left with a used car that he had already sold once only to then buy back in order to personally prove it was worthless.

So Exactly When Are You Allowed To Exceed The Legal Speed Limit?

According to a representative of the UK Magistrates Association's road traffic committee:

'The only people who are statutorily allowed to speed are drivers of the emergency service vehicles when going about proper business.'

However anyone caught speeding can opt to go before the Magistrates' Court where they can try offering 'special reasons' in their defence. If a doctor has been caught speeding while going to an emergency this is usually considered a good excuse.

Traffic police are also allowed to show discretion. Home Office Guidance on the Operation of the Fixed Penalty System for Offences in Respect of a Vehicle police forces are advised:

'An officer will at all times consider the circumstances of the offence when reaching a decision whether to take no further action, give a verbal warning... complete a FPN (fixed penalty notice) or report for summons, bearing in mind any mitigating or exacerbating factors which may be present. At all times police action must be seen to be fair, consistent and proportionate, requiring the same standard of evidence for the issue of a FPN as required for a court hearing.'

The Juggling Lane

A juggler is driving to a performance when he gets stopped by the police. The police man is suspicious of all the matches and tins of lighter fluid on the back seat. The juggler therefore has to demonstrate his act for the policeman and stands at the side of the road juggling a set of flaming torches. Just at that moment Gerald and Thelma drive past. 'Will you look at that,' says Gerald to his wife. 'Thank God I stopped drinking. Just look at the test the police make you do these days!'

An Easy Mistake To Make

Two old ladies go out in their large car, both of them barely managing to peer over the dashboard. They get to a junction and go through a red light. The old lady in the passenger seat, thinks, 'I swear we just went through a red light.' A few minutes later they go through another red light and again the old lady is almost sure that the light was red, but wonders if she might be mistaken. At the next junction they go through another red light and she turns to her friend and says, 'Did you know we just went through three red lights in a row! You could have killed us!' 'Oh no!' says her friend looking around alarmed. 'I didn't realise I was the one driving!'

Another Great Way
To Evade A Speeding Fine

In 2005, chartered surveyors Stewart and Cathryn Bromley received two £60 fines for speeding in Dukinfield Road, Hyde, Greater Manchester.

And so the Bromleys did what anyone else would do in the circumstances. They invented a fictitious Bulgarian and claimed that he had been the one who had been driving their Mercedes at the time of the speeding incidents.

The Bulgarian was, Mr Bromley explained to police, a former employee of theirs called Konstantin Koscov. Unfortunately it was not possible for Mr Koscov to come forward and take the rap for his speeding offence because by this time he had gone back to his native Bulgaria.

Nevertheless the Bromleys could prove their story was true. After returning home to Bulgaria, Mr Koscov had gone to the trouble of sending the Bromleys a postcard decorated with scenic Bulgarian images. Even more helpfully Mr Koscov had in his postcard expressly thanked the Bromleys for the use of their car and noted the high performance of which it was capable.

The police did what any other force pursuing a £60 speeding ticket would have done. They got Interpol involved and contacted the British Embassy in Sofia. Sure enough the mysterious Konstantin Koscov turned out not to exist.

The postcard had in fact been sent by Mrs Bromley herself. She had flown 1,400 miles to Bulgaria to post a picture postcard back to herself in an attempt to incriminate the fictitious Konstantin Koscov.

The Bromleys were fined £9,200 and ordered to pay £1,900 costs after they pleaded guilty to perverting the course of justice.

Oh well! At least one of them got a brief trip to Bulgaria out of it!

Another Top Tip
If You Get Caught Speeding

A police officer pulls a speeding female driver over. 'Is there some sort of problem, officer?' she asks him. 'You were speeding, madam,' says the policeman. 'May I see your licence?' 'I'm sorry,' says the woman. 'I don't have a licence. I have been banned four times as a result of drunk driving.' 'OK,' says the officer. 'Do you have your vehicle registration documents?' 'Sorry,' says the woman. 'I don't have those either. I stole this car, killed the owner and stuffed his remains in the boot.' The horrified policeman immediately calls for back-up and suddenly five other police cars have circled the woman. The local Chief Constable slowly approaches and calls, 'Madam, could you open the back of your car please.' She does so revealing the boot to be empty. 'Is this your car?' asks the Chief Constable. 'Oh yes,' says the woman. 'Here are the registration documents.' The Chief Constable is confused. 'I was told that you don't have a driving licence.' The woman digs into her handbag and pulls out her licence. 'This is all very strange,' says the Chief Constable. 'My officer told me that you didn't have a licence, that you stole this car, and that you'd murdered the owner.' 'I don't believe it!' exclaims the woman. 'Next you'll tell me the lying bastard said I was speeding as well.'

Excuses Given By Drivers Caught Speeding

My son/daughter was ill in the back of the car and I was rushing to a doctor. (Photographic evidence showed that a female passenger was asleep in the front of the car – there was no sick child!)

My colon has fallen into my vaginal canal.

My colonoscopy bag is leaking (The driver went on to prove that this was in fact the case to the police officer who had stopped him. The police officer told the driver to 'Have a nice night')

As I entered onto the motorway, my car was dragged along in the slipstream of a truck. My brakes aren't very good, so I had to keep pace with it.

I had to drive that fast because it was the only way I could get the windscreen to de-mist so I could see out.

Speeding Between Two Wives

In 2008, Scottish restaurant owner Mohammed Anwar was charged with driving at 64 mph in a 30 mph zone in Falkirk.

A court allowed Mr Anwar to keep his licence after he explained he needed it because he had two wives. One of Mr Anwar's wives lived in Motherwell, the other in Glasgow. Mr Anwar slept with each of his wives on a simple rota system travelling between them on alternate nights. Mr Anwar thus successfully argued that he needed to keep his driving licence in order to carry on fulfilling his matrimonial duties.

It remained unclear however which of his wives he was travelling to and which away from at the time he was clocked doing twice the speed limit.

Monte Carlo Or Bust

Perhaps the best-known car rally in the world, the Monte Carlo Rally started in 1911 and is still going strong today. No, the 1911 race is not still going, you understand, although competitors may sometimes be forgiven for thinking they have embarked on something interminable. The 2009 rally lasted from January 21 to 24, and the rules allow a whole week to finish the course. And it can be pretty dangerous, what with mountain roads, hairpin bends, and onlookers sometimes chucking ice and snow on the road to liven things up a bit. In 2009, 47 teams began the race, but only 29 finished.

Those Daring Young Men In Their Jaunty Jalopies

That was the American title of *Monte Carlo Or Bust*, a 1969 film based on the Monte Carlo Rally. It starred Tony Curtis, Peter Cook, Dudley Moore and Susan Hampshire. The American title was of course an allusion to an earlier film by the same team (and some of the same cast) entitled *Those Magnificent Men In Their Flying Machines*. We are still awaiting the third in the trilogy, *Those Perishing Prats On Their Pizza-delivery Mopeds*.

Is It A Car, Is It A Plane?

The current holder of the world land speed record is Briton Andy Green, who achieved a staggering 763 mph in the Thrust SSC car on October 15 1997. He not only broke the world record, he broke the sound barrier too. The car was British designed and British built (by Richard Noble who held the previous record of 633 mph with Thrust 2 from 1983), setting the record at black Rock Desert USA. The car was twin turbofan powered. The turbofan engine is more usually used for aeroplanes, and fittingly the driver, Andy Green, was an RAF pilot. Perhaps the most amazing thing about this record is that the vehicle actually managed to stay on the ground!

Whatever Next?

The Americans, naturally, do not wish to stand idly by watching the land speed records being set and then smashed by us damn Limeys, especially as we rub their noses in it by going and setting the records over there in the US of A, so...

They have a team of engineers busy converting (get this!) a Lockheed F-104 jet fighter into the North American Eagle, a vehicle capable of achieving 800 mph.

But the Brits won't stand for that surely? No, they won't. Richard Noble and his boys are working on the Bloodhound SSC, a three-engined monster with which they hope to achieve 1,000 mph in 2011. Let's hope they remember to clunk click before they set off.

The 1,000 mph Car

The final design for the UK's 1,000 mph car was settled in November 2009.

The original plan had been to position a 200 kg rocket above a 1,000kg Eurofighter Typhoon jet engine. During the car's development however it became clear that additional thrust was needed to overcome the aerodynamic drag. So the team had to send out for a 400kg rocket instead.

It then turned out that having the jet engine underneath was, according to the car's chief designer, causing 'some quite high lift loads at the rear end of the car.' Well, it probably would now you come to think of it!

The cunning solution was to position the jet engine above the rocket. The Bloodhound is expected to start running in 2011 on a site in Northern Cape Province, South Africa.

It would of course be difficult to test a 1,000 mph car in the United Kingdom itself as the total distance from Land's End to John O'Groats is only 874 miles. And besides, the traffic lights along the way might hold you up a bit.

British Land Speed Records

February 4, 1927
Malcolm Campbell drove the Napier-Campbell Bluebird at 174.883 mph (281.447 kph) on the beach at Pendine Sands, a 7 mile beach on the shores of Carmarthen Bay in South Wales.

March 11, 1929
Major Henry Seagrave set a land speed record of 231.446 mph (372.340 kph) at Daytona Beach, Florida in the Golden Arrow 1,000 horsepower Sunbeam at. The car had done just 18.74 miles when it set the record. It thus set another record for being the least used car used to set the land speed record. Seagrave was killed a year later setting the water speed record at Lake Windermere.

September 3, 1935
Malcolm Campbell averaged a speed of 301.129 mph (484.818 kph) at the Bonneville Salt Flats, Utah in the Campbell Rolls-Royce Bluebird. Campbell died in 1948 from a series of strokes. He was one of the few land speed record holders of his era to die from natural causes.

November 19, 1937
Captain George Eyston set a record of 312.00 mph at the Bonneville Salt Flats, Utah in Thunderbolt, a 73 litre, twin Rolls Royce engined vehicle.

August 27, 1938
Eyston raised the record to 345.50 mph (556.03 kph).

September 15, 1938
John R Cobb achieved 353.30 mph (568.58 kph) in the Railton Special.

September 16, 1938
Eyston must have been extremely put out by Cobb's record! Less than 24 hours after Cobb set his record, Eyston recorded a speed of 357.50 mph (575.34 kph).

August 23, 1939
Cobb took the record back again with a speed of 369.70 mph (594.97 kph).

September 16, 1947
Cobb drove the Railton Mobil Special at Bonneville Salt Flats and set a new record of 394.196 mph (634.196 kph). He had however been attempting to break 400 mph. Cobb died in 1952 attempting the water speed record on Loch Ness.

July 17, 1964
Donald Campbell achieved 403.10 mph (648.73 kph) in the Bluebird-Proteus CN7 at Lake Eyre, Australia. It was Campbell's only foray into the land speed record. He died attempting the water speed record on Coniston Water in January 1967.

October 4, 1983
In the Black Rock Desert, Nevada, Richard Noble drove the jet propelled Thrust 2 at an average speed of 633.468 mph (1,019.468 kph). If he had gone just 7 mph faster, the vehicle would have become airborne resulting in certain death.

October 15, 1997
Thrust SSC (Supersonic Car) driven by Andy Green achieved 763 mph (1,228 kph) in the Black Rock Desert. Thrust SSC was the first car to break the sound barrier, the speed of sound being estimated to be around 740 mph.

WISE WORDS FOR THE CAR BUYER

You have decided to buy a car. Immediately you run into the difficulty which faces most people: you probably have some idea of the type of car you want, and now you must find out whether or not you can afford it.

Nobody can advise you about that. You alone know how much you have to spend. But remember that the man who is selling you the car will be pleased if he can get more of your money than you intended to give him.

Practical Car Owner Illustrated, 1955

The First Motor Show

Britain's First Motor Show was snappily titled the Horseless Carriage Exhibition of 1895. It was organised by RAC founder member Sir Evelyn Ellis and held in a field at Tunbridge Wells where just five vehicles were exhibited: two cars, a fire engine, a steam carriage and a tricycle. A mere 500 people attended. Well, what did they expect? How was anyone supposed to get there when there were so few cars around?

The first British Motor Show was held at Crystal Palace from January 30 to February 7, 1903. This time 10,000 people attended which was pretty good going seeing as there were only 8,000 private cars on the road at the time.

The 1912 British Motor Show catalogue listed 165 different makes of car. The most expensive car listed was a Napier, 90 horse power four-seater vehicle costing £1,840. At the other end of the market, the cheapest car available was a two-seater Humberette costing just £95.

Take most people, they're crazy about cars. They worry if they get a little scratch on them, and they're always talking about how many miles they get to a gallon, and if they get a brand-new car already they start thinking about trading it in for one that's even newer. I don't even like old cars. I mean they don't even interest me. I'd rather have a goddam horse. A horse is at least human, for God's sake.

J.D. Salinger (Catcher in the Rye)

Buying A Car

Half the art of buying a car is learning to read between the lines. So whatever the ads tell you, the interesting bit is what they don't tell you. For example:

One careful owner (all the rest were maniacs)

Low mileage (the odometer is in kilometres)

Drives like a dream (a nightmare is a sort of a dream isn't it?)

It's a steal (I nicked it)

Full service history (the last full service was back in history)

Nice little runaround (That's what I'll give you if you ask for a refund)

To attract men, I wear a perfume called 'New Car Interior'.

Rita Rudner

My boyfriend keeps telling me I've got to own things. So, first I bought this car. And then he told me I oughta get a house. 'Why a house?' 'Well, you gotta have a place to park the car.'

Julia Roberts

Have you heard about the Irishman who reversed into a car boot sale and sold the engine?

Frank Carson

The New Car

When a family buys a new car everyone has a different attitude to it:

Dad says, 'I wonder how many miles it does to the gallon.'

Mum says, 'I wonder what colour the upholstery is.'

The daughter says, 'I wonder how good the mirror is.'

The son says, 'I wonder how fast it'll go.'

And the next door neighbour says, 'I wonder where the hell those idiots got the money from!'

The Cheapest Cars In The World

In January 2008 the Tata Nano car was unveiled in India. The price was 100,000 rupees, which sounds quite a lot, but in pounds comes to around £1,300. The most expensive, incidentally, is the Bugatti Veyron which could perhaps be renamed 'Tata to over a million pounds.'

Prior to the emergence of the Tata Nano the cheapest new cars in the world were the Chinese QQ3 Chery and the Indian Maruti M800 which would each have set you back around £2,500.

All this puts one in mind of the heyday of the Model T Ford, which in 1925 would have cost just $290 – and you got a lot more dollars for your pound in those days!

People don't want cheap cars. They want expensive cars that cost less!

Amazing!

The Office for National Statistics (ONS) has some fascinating data regarding motor cars. According to the ONS, between 1971 and 2007 the proportion of households in Great Britain with access to a car went up from 52 per cent to 75 per cent.

It also tells us that, remarkably, over the same period, the proportion of households without access to a car went down from 48 per cent to 25 per cent!

It's good to know that someone is keeping track of all this.

The Number of Cars on UK Roads

In 1904 there were 8,000 cars in Britain.

In 1910 there were 124,860 'light motor cars' on UK roads.

By 1930 there were over one million cars on the road

In 1950, the figure was two million.

By 1959 there were over 5 million

In 1961 the number of cars had leapt up to 10 million

By 1970 we were up to 15 million

By 1983 it was 20 million

In 2007 a survey showed there to be 31,105,988.

Short Cuts

I have a rented car, which is a flat rate 12 cents a mile. In an effort to cut down on the mileage charge, I back up every place.

Woody Allen

Car designers are just going to have to come up with an automobile that outlasts the payments.

Erma Bombeck

John is looking at a second hand car. He asks the salesman, 'Why is this car covered in dents? I thought you said it had had one careful owner.' 'That's true, it did,' replies the salesman. 'But unfortunately the rest weren't very careful at all.'

The Used Car Market

In 2008 sales in the second hand car market in the UK amounted to around £35 billion.

The level of fraud was also said to be huge with the cost of car clocking alone being estimated to be £100 million per year.

In a recent survey of gripes among UK consumers, complaints against second hand car dealers topped the poll. And not for the first time!

Government-funded advice service Consumer Direct announced in 2009 that they had received a total of 874,171 consumer complaint cases during the year. Of these 47,019 complaints had related to independent used car traders. This figure had increased by 7% over the previous twelve months. And it didn't even include complaints about second hand cars bought from franchises! These were in at number 6 on the same list of top ten complaints!

In total sixty eight thousand people had complained to Consumer Direct about second hand cars in 2009. Meanwhile across the Irish Sea, the Irish National Consumer Agency reported that they had received a total of 3,815 complaints during the first half of 2009. Of these a staggering 73% (2,800 complaints) related to second hand vehicles. The Irish National Consumer Agency did however go on to say that many of the vehicles involved in these figures must have entered Ireland from the UK. Well, that should help international relations!

The main issues leading to complaints highlighted by the National Consumer Agency were:

Used cars that later proved to be faulty or repeatedly broke down.

Second hand cars sold as having one previous owner when in fact there may have been several.

Incorrect mileage recorded.

Cars that had been involved in a crash about which the buyer had not been informed of at the time of purchase.

Second hand cars sold with finance still outstanding on them .

There is a crisis in America. That crisis is divorce. It is easier to get out of a marriage than [to get out of a] contract to buy a used car.

Mike Huckabee

Jack bought a second-hand car. It had had just one previous owner. A little old lady who only used it once a week on Sundays... to go out drag racing.

Just One Previous Owner

A man goes to buy a second-hand car. His eye is taken by one vehicle in particular. 'Nice car that,' says the dealer. 'Just one previous owner. A sweet little 85-year-old lady who only ever drove it once a week over to her sister's house half a mile away.' The man is impressed and takes a closer look. A couple of minutes later, he asks the salesman, 'Did you say this car only had one previous 85-year-old lady owner?' 'Yes,' says the salesman. 'What's the problem? Don't you believe me?' 'Of course,' says the man, handing the salesman a plastic bag. 'It's just that she left a packet of condoms, a porn mag and a bottle of aftershave in the glove compartment and I wondered if she might want them back.'

Second Hand Cars

There are certain things to look out for when buying a second hand car. Here a few:

1. Look in the mirror just to check that you haven't got the word 'Mug' emblazoned across your forehead.
2. Check the bodywork for telltale signs of previous crashes – e.g. someone has crudely painted the word 'ouch!' next to a large dent.
3. Check the mileage. A 1962 Mini with just 1400 miles on the clock may indicate either an unusually long line of 'little old lady' owners, or just one crook.
4. Do a dipstick test. That is, seeing if dipstick comes out covered in black gunk rather than simply looking at yourself in the car mirror to see if you look like a sucker.
5. Check the engine. Even if you know nothing at all about engines, just lifting the bonnet and poking around while making sucking noises through your teeth and tutting occasionally may just convince the seller that you do know something.
6. Kick the tyres. Again, you may have no idea why you are doing this, but it seems to be par for the course from people who do know the first thing about cars.
7. Check the car registration documents and see if the name on those is the same as the person selling you the car. Though if they are both Mr M. Mouse proceed with caution.
8. Look out for funny bumper stickers. Would you want to buy a car from somebody with a twisted sense of humour?
9. Check what station the car radio is tuned to. You may be safer buying a car from a Radio 3 listener than one who regularly tunes in to Headbanger FM.
10. Check that price again. If it's a bargain then it probably isn't a bargain.

Happy hunting!

ABSOLUTE CLASSICS!

Motor Companies That Began Manufacture In The 19th Century

Bollee (France) 1873

Benz (Germany) 1885

Panhard Et Levassor (France) 1889

Peugeot (France) 1889

Delahaye (France) 1894

Lanchester (England) 1895

Oldsmobile (USA) 1896

Daimler (England) 1897

Humber (England) 1898

Opel (Germany) 1898

Renault (France) 1898

Riley (England) 1898

Austro-Daimler (Austria) 1899

Packard (USA) 1899

Fiat (Italy) 1899

Sunbeam (England) 1899

Wolseley (England) 1899

The Tin Lizzie

Henry Ford's 'car for the great multitude', the Model T, was first put into production on September 27, 1908. It had a 20-horse power, four cylinder engine. It could reach a top speed of 45 mph and did 13 to 21 miles per gallon of fuel.

Ford's often misquoted line about the car was: 'Any customer can have a car painted any colour that he wants so long as it is black.'

In fact the Model T was available in other colours apart from black between 1908 and 1914 and again between 1926 and 1927.

Over 15 million Model Ts were built and by 1916, 55% of all the cars in the world were Model Ts. The car was originally priced at $850 although this was later reduced to as little as $260, for a model without extras, because of production savings which Ford was able to pass on to customers.

The Ford Model A had been the first car produced by the Ford Motor Company. The first Model A was purchased by Chicago dentist Dr Ernst Pfenning on July 23, 1903. Unfortunately by the time of this first sale, the Ford company only had $223.65 remaining out of an initial $28,000 in assets. As you may be aware however after this things picked up for the company.

The Model A was followed by the Model B and the Model C in 1904, Model F in 1905, the Model N in 1906, the Model R and the Model S in 1907. What Ford had against the letters, D, E, G, H, I, J, K, L, M, O, P and Q is not known.

What's more, Ford followed up the Model T in 1928 with the Model A. It was, he said, such a departure from the Model T that it was best to start all over again.

Spying a gap in the market, the rival Chrysler corporation marketed a car called the Model U in 1928 although this was soon renamed the Plymouth.

The Spirit of Ecstasy

The Rolls Royce hood ornament is called The Spirit of Ecstasy. The woman who modelled for the emblem was Eleanor Velasco Thornton, the mistress of Lord Montagu of Beaulieu. It was this relationship that led not only to her being immortalised as the Rolls Royce emblem but also to her untimely death at the age of 35.

Eleanor was born in Stockwell in 1880 to a Spanish mother and an Australian engineer. She left school at 16 and worked for the Automobile Club (subsequently the RAC). Through her work she met many pioneers of the early motoring industry including the Conservative MP, John Walter Edward Douglas-Scott-Montagu, the future second Baron Montagu of Beaulieu.

She became Montagu's mistress and worked as his assistant on *The Car Illustrated*, Britain's first motoring magazine. In 1903 the couple had an illegitimate daughter, Joan, whom Eleanor had to give up for adoption.

In 1910 Claude Goodman Johnson, the first Managing Director of Rolls Royce Limited, commissioned Charles Sykes to create a radiator mascot that would be 'something beautiful, like Nike.' That's the 2,000 year old marble statue of Nike, the Goddess of Victory in the Louvre Museum in case you were wondering why Rolls Royce cars don't have a silver training shoe balanced over the radiator.

Sykes was a regular illustrator for *The Car Illustrated* and Eleanor Thornton had become his favourite model. Inspiration for the Spirit of Ecstasy came probably during a ride in Montagu's Rolls Royce on the road from London to Beaulieu. According to Sykes' daughter, the sculptor was 'very impressed with the smoothness and speed of the car, and imagined that even so delicate a thing as a fairy could ride on the bonnet without losing her balance.'

From 1911 every Rolls of Royce came with a Spirit of Ecstasy. At first they were silver plated, each individual one was signed and dated by Charles Sykes and no two figures were exactly alike. Henry Royce however did not like the emblem and thus rarely drove his car with the figure in place.

Eleanor Thornton lost her life while sailing to India with Lord Montagu. Their ship the SS Persia was torpedoed off Crete on 30th December 1915. In five minutes the vessel sank with the loss of 343 of its 510 passengers. As the ship tipped over Eleanor and Montagu were washed into the sea. Montagu managed to get to the surface and reached a badly damaged lifeboat on which he drifted for more than 30 hours. Eleanor however was never found.

Audi You Do

Audi's name is sometimes incorrectly said to stand for Auto Union Deutschland Ingolstadt. The founder of the company August Horch had been forced out of his original business in 1909. He then began a new car production company but was prevented from using his own name for the business as this now legally belonged to his previous organisation. Horch means 'to hear' in German. So instead of calling his cars Horch, they derived their new name from the Latin 'to hear' ('audio').

Motor Companies That Began Manufacture Between 1900 And The First World War

Mercedes (Germany) 1901	Singer (England) 1905
Cadillac (USA) 1902	Lancia (Italy) 1906
Studebaker (USA) 1902	Austin (England) 1906
Ford (USA) 1903	AC (England) 1908
Talbot (England) 1903	Audi (Germany) 1909
Vauxhall (England) 1903	Bugatti (France) 1909
Buick (USA) 1904	Alfa Romeo (Italy) 1910
Rolls Royce (England) 1904	Chevrolet (USA) 1911
Rover (England) 1904	Morris (England) 1913
Delage (France) 1905	Dodge (USA) 1914

I couldn't find the sports car of my dreams, so I built it myself.
Ferdinand Porsche

Durant Durant

Crapo is an unusual name to give a child. He wasn't even one of the more popular members of the Marx Brothers. Crapo was however the middle name of the founder of General Motors, William Crapo Durant.

Durant had begun as a cigar salesman before making his fortune making horse-drawn vehicles in the late 1800s. He thought the new fangled cars were smelly and dangerous and refused to let his daughter ride in one. Nevertheless in 1904 he took over the Buick Company who had up until this point produced just 37 cars. After entering a Buick in a New York auto show, Durant returned with 1,108 orders.

General Motors was founded on September 16, 1908 with Oldsmobile, Pontiac and Cadillac then quickly being merged into the company. A group of stockholders ousted Durant from the company in 1911. Five years later he regained control of the company using profits from the car he had gone on to produce, the Chevrolet.

By 1954, GM had sold 50 million cars in less than 50 years and had 54% of the US car market. The following year GM became the first US company to pay a tax bill of $1 billion.

For 77 years GM was the world's bestselling motor manufacturer but lost the title to Toyota in 2008. By the end of March 2009 the recession-hit GM announced it had debts of $172 billion against $82 billion of assets and was forced to file for bankruptcy soon afterwards.

Luckily though Durant had never insisted his name be given to any of his company's cars and so the world was spared, for example, the Vauxhall Crapo.

The Jewish Beetle

The Volkswagen is famous as the peoples' car. Ferdinand Porsche
worked on the design with advice from none other than German
leader, Adolf Hitler.

Hitler ordered Porsche to develop a 'volks-wagen', which
would cost less than 1,000 Reichsmark. The first 30 pilot cars
were constructed by Daimler Benz in 1937. At this stage the car
was called the Porsche Type 60 or the KdF-Wagen. And that's KdF
in the sense of *Kraft Durche Freude* or in other words the Strength
Through Joy Mobile!

Hitler laid the foundation of the Volkswagen factory at
Wolfsburg in 1938 and the car became nicknamed the Kuafer (or
Beetle). Unlike its Nazi progenitor, the Beetle went on to conquer
the world becoming the most successful car in motoring history.

So if nothing else good can be said about him was Hitler a
visionary of the car industry? Or might he have just stolen the idea
for the Volkswagen off a Jew? According to Paul Schilperoord's
book *Het Ware Verhaal van de Kever* ('The True Story of the
Beetle'), the original idea for the Volkswagen was indeed first
dreamed up by a Jewish engineer, Josef Ganz.

Ganz had been working from 1923 on a light, simple,
inexpensive car that the average German citizen could afford.
He called his concept the volks-wagen and in 1930 and 1931
built two prototypes of a car called the Maikäfer (May-Beetle).
Ganz developed the Maikäfer as the Standard Superior. A 1934
brochure for the Standard Superior has on its cover an illustration
of a car that looks remarkably like the future VW beetle as well
as the phrase 'Deutschen Volkswagen'. Guess what! Hitler had
seen the Standard Superior in 1934. He liked the design but not its
Jewish designer so much.

Ganz was arrested by the Gestapo in May 1933 and after
his release survived two assassination attempts. Ganz escaped
to Switzerland. After many years trying to stake his claim to the
Volkswagen concept, he died in obscurity in Australia in 1967.

Sieur de Cadillac

The Cadillac motor company had originally been the Henry Ford Company. In 1903 Ford left the company following a dispute with his financiers but was allowed to take his name and $800. Ford went on to found the Ford Motor Company while his old business was left to find itself a new name.

Cadillac was named after the French explorer Antoine Laumet de la Mothe, Sieur de Cadillac. In 1701 Cadillac had founded Fort Pontchartrain du Détroit or Fort Détroit. This eventually became the city of Detroit and the centre of the United States motor industry.

In The Beginning Was The Logo

Audi
Audi's four ring logo symbolises the merger in 1932 of four independent motor manufacturers into one new company. The four companies who merged were Audi, DKW, Horch and Wanderer. After the war the name Audi disappeared until it was revived in 1965.

BMW
The BMW logo is not, as many believe, meant to represent a propeller. The logo was however used in a 1929 advertisement promoting the company's radial aero engines. Nevertheless the blue and white quadrants of the logo in fact depict the official colours of Bavaria. And of course Bavaria is the home of Bayerische Motoren Werke!

Citroen
Citroen's 'double chevron' logo is a reference to gear teeth and André Citroën's early involvement in the gear-cutting industry.

Lamborgini

The Lamborghini logo depicts a bull referring to the astrological sign Taurus, this being the birth sign of the company's founder, Ferruccio Lamborghini.

Mercedes Benz

The Mercedes Benz logo is said to depict a star in a circle and to date from the time in 1872 when Gottlieb Daimler was working at the Deutz gas engine factory in Cologne. Daimler sent his wife, Emma, a picture postcard of the city on which he marked the house in which he was living with a three-pointed star. He told her that 'one day this star will shine over our triumphant factories.' After his death in 1900, Daimler's sons, Paul and Adolf, suggested using the star as the company's symbol. The proposal was accepted in 1909. The company also registered a symbol incorporating a four pointed star although this has never been used.

Mitsubishi

The name Mitsubishi combines two Japanese words, 'mitsu' and 'hishi'. 'Mitsu' means three and 'hishi' (pronunciation of which is different from spelling) means water chestnut although for a long time it has been used to refer to a diamond shape. So hence Mitsubishi's three diamond logo.

Peugeot

The Peugeot lion symbol was originally introduced to mark saw blades manufactured by the company in the days before cars had even been invented. The lion was said to symbolise three essential qualities of Peugeot's saw blades: toughness, flexibility and speed.

Subaru

In Japanese the star cluster Pleiades is called Subaru. The company's logo shows one large star and five smaller stars, referring to the five Japanese companies that merged in 1953 to form Fuji Heavy Industries, of which Subaru is the automotive component.

Vauxhall

Vauxhall's logo depicts a griffin, a mythical creature that is part eagle and part lion. The emblem derives from the coat of arms of Faulke de Breaute, a mercenary soldier to whom King John granted the Manor of Luton. He also gained rights to an area south of the Thames in London where the name of his house, Fulk's Hall, eventually became Vauxhall. The griffin symbol was used by Vauxhall Iron Works who coincidentally moved out to Luton in 1905.

Volvo

Volvo's logo represents a circle with an arrow this being the symbol for iron.

What They Say Those Car Acronyms Really Stand For...

AMC – Another Major Catastrophe

AUDI – Another Ugly Deutsche Invention

BMW – Breaks Most Wrenches

BUICK – Big Ugly Import Car Killer

CADILLAC – Cars Are Driven In Long Lines and Crashed

CHEVROLET – Cheap, Hardly Efficient, Virtually Runs On Luck Every Time

DODGE – Dead On Day Guarantee Expires

EDSEL – Every Day Something Else Leaks

FIAT – Fix It Again, Tony!

FORD – Fast Only Rolling Downhill

HONDA – Had One, Never Did Again

HYUNDAI – How Your Usual Nerd Drives An Import

JAGUAR – Junk Always Going Under At Repair Shop

KIA – Killed In Action

LOTUS – Lots of Trouble Usually Serious

M.G. – Money Guzzler

MAZDA – Made At Zoo by Demented Apes

MERCEDES – Most Eccentric Rich Capitalists Enjoy Driving Expensive Sedans

PONTIAC – Puts Out Noxious Toxins In All Cities

PORSCHE – Proof Of Rich Spoiled Children Having Everything

SAAB – Send Another Automobile Back

SUBARU – Screwed Up Beyond All Repair Usually

TOYOTA – The One You Ought To Avoid

TRIU MPH – Tried Repairing It Until My Pants Hurt

VOLVO – Very Odd Looking Vehicular Object

VW – Virtually Worthless

I have a BMW. But only because BMW stands for Bob Marley and the Wailers, and not because I need an expensive car.

Bob Marley

Motor Companies Beginning Manufacture Between The Wars

Armstrong Siddeley (England) 1919

Citroen (France) 1919

Alvis (England) 1920

Bentley (England) 1920

Lincoln (USA) 1920

Aston Martin (England) 1922

MG (England) 1923

Tatra (Czechoslovakia) 1923

Triumph (England) 1923

Chrysler (USA) 1924

Skoda (Czechoslovakia) 1924

Maserati (Italy) 1926

Pontiac (USA) 1926

Mercedes Benz (Germany) 1926

Volvo (Sweden) 1927

BMW (Germany) 1928

Plymouth (USA) 1928

Datsun (later Nissan) (Japan) 1931

Volkswagen (Germany) 1938

Toyota (Japan) 1935

The Saviour of Volkswagen

The survival of Volkswagen after the end of the Second World War was largely due to an Englishman, Ivan Hirst.

In 1945 Hirst was a major in the Royal Electrical and Mechanical Engineers. He was given the job of running a workshop for British army vehicles in the ruined Volkswagen plant at Wolfsburg. Originally the idea was to dismantle the factory but when the German production equipment was offered to British motor companies such as Rootes and Morris, they turned it down. The Volkswagen Beetle would have been, according to an official British report 'a completely uneconomic enterprise.' And it's that kind of foresight that has made the British car manufacturing industry what it is today!

Instead Hirst helped get production going again at Wolfsburg by clearing the bomb damage and re-commissioning production equipment. He also helped improve the design of the beetle and set up a sales and service network for Volkswagen.

In January 1949 the running of the company was handed over to former Opel production manager, Heinrich Nordhoff. Over the next 20 years under Nordfhoff, Volkswagen became one of the world's leading car manufacturers but without Hirst, the name, badge and aesthetic of Volkswagen could have been lost forever.

Motor Companies Beginning Manufacture Post Second World War

Jaguar (England) 1945

Ferrari (Italy) 1946

Lotus (England) 1947

Porsche (Austria) 1948

Saab (Sweden) 1949

American Motors Corporation (USA) 1954

TVR (England) 1954

Mazda (Japan) 1960

Honda (Japan) 1962

Lamborghini (Italy) 1963

Lada (Russia) 1970

Hyundai (Korea) 1974

Daewoo (Korea) 1980

Kia (Korea) 1986

Land Roving Through Anglesey

The Land Rover was first developed by Rover designer Maurice Wilks at his farm in Newborough, Anglesey in 1948. Land Rovers were originally sage green because this colour paint was available from a fighter plane factory.

It was once claimed that 75% of all the Land Rovers ever made were still in use.

The E-Type Swallow Sidecar

The first car to bear the Jaguar name was made in 1935 and cost £395. Jaguars might not seem such desirable cars if their manufacturer had stuck with its original name: The Swallow Sidecar Company.

Dearly Remembered Cars

Ain't it strange that three of Britain's most dearly remembered cars were designed by a Greek? Alexander Arnold Constantine Issigonis was born in Smyrna, part of the Ottoman Empire, in 1906 and moved to the UK in 1923. So, what were the cars?

Morris Minor

One of Britain's favourite ever cars. These rolled off the production line in 1948 and continued being manufactured until 1971. They were intended to be affordable motors for ordinary working people and 1.6 million were made. There is still a Morris Minor Owners' Club which boasts 14,500 members around the world.

Mini

Almost as synonymous with the 1960s as the Beatles, this iconic motor actually began at the tail end of the 1950s in 1959 and again was designed by Alec Issigonis. It continued production to 2000. The sporty models, Mini Cooper and Cooper S won the Monte Carlo rally in 1964, 1965 and 1967. The Mini Moke was manufactured between 1964 and 1968 and achieved immortality and cult status in the TV series The Prisoner. Forty years on there is still a Mini Moke Club in existence

ADO 16

Never heard of it? Ok, ADO 16 was the code name under which it was manufactured (Austin Drawing Office design number 16). It later became known as the Austin 1100, and was the third of the much-loved British cars made by Alec Issigonnis. Mark 1 was manufactured between 1962 and 1967, Mark II from 1967-71 and Mark III from 1971-74. In 1985 the 1100 Club was formed for enthusiasts of BMC 1100-1300 cars.

The Bubble Car

German manufacturer Messerschmitt produced the majority of fighter aircraft for the Nazis during first half of the Second World War. Following the war the company was banned from producing aeroplanes. They therefore had to diversify into car production and they came up with a very odd vehicle indeed.

The design for Messerschmitt's car was based on that of an invalid carriage which is probably not a good start if you're aiming to create an exciting, sexy, high performance automobile. Former Luftwaffe technical officer Fritz Fend had produced 250 of his Fend Flitzer three wheeler invalid carriages when he discovered that many of them were not being bought by invalids at all. Instead able bodied people were buying them to use as a basic means of transport.

The Flitzer design was adapted for mass production for Messerschmitt. And so the world was given the bubble car. And as befitted the bastard offspring of the designer of the Fend Flitzer and an aircraft manufacturer, the car did indeed seem to comprise a small aircraft canopy balanced on the chassis of an invalid carriage. Messerschmitt's aeronautical tendencies were further indicated by the fact that the car could carry just two people, one sitting behind the other.

Messerschmitt's KR175 was in production from 1953 to 1955 and the KR200 (the Kabinenroller) from 1956 to 1964. After 1964 production ceased. Somewhat ironically the recovery of the German economy proved disastrous for Messerschmitt. Demand for the company's cars fell as the country's population grew wealthier and became able to afford cars that had 4 rather than 3 wheels.

But if only Messerschmitt had been restricted to producing bubble cars during the war. It might have made the Battle of Britain a briefer and simpler operation.

BMW similarly got in on the act with the Isetta. The Isetta had originally been an Italian design and was an extraordinarily compact car at 7.5 feet long by 4.5 feet wide. It was one of the world's few cars to follow the example of washing machines by being a front loader with the door in front of the driver's seat. The steering wheel and instrument panel swung out with the door allowing access to the car's single bench seat.

Spitting Feathers

According to legend a number of Minis kept breaking down in the early 1960s. Eventually the fault was traced to mysterious red hairs clogging the carburettor. These in turn were traced to a red feather duster that was being used by one of the cleaning ladies on the Mini production line at Cowley, Oxford!

Reliant Robin

Not Robin Reliant as many people say. This car largely has a place in our affections because of its use in Only Fools and Horses. The only problem is that Del Boy never drove a Reliant Robin, he drove a Reliant Regal van. Still, as the Reliant Robin has also been the butt of many affectionate jokes over the years we don't mind about such details. It was first manufactured in 1966 and continued production until 1981 – just about the time Only Fools and Horses was starting off, Lovely Jubbly!

Austin Seven

One of the most popular British cars ever and manufactured between 1922 and 1939. 290,000 were made, which may not sound such a large number today, but this was in what were then the relatively early days of motoring. There are many Austin Seven clubs and they have now formed together under the umbrella Austin Seven Clubs Association.

Mini Hatred

The Mini was developed because the head of the British Motor Corporation, Leonard Lord, hated three wheeled bubble cars. 'God damn these bloody awful bubble cars,' said Lord. 'We must drive them out of the streets by designing a proper miniature car.' In response Alec Issigonis designed a car with room for four passengers in an overall car length of just 10 feet. His original doodle of the car was literally done on the back of a cigarette packet. Perhaps if he'd been a cigar smoker, he would have come up with a bigger car!

Rockin' Corolla

The best-selling car of all time is the Toyota Corolla. The Corolla was first introduced in Japan in 1966. Australia was the destination for the first Corolla to be exported from Japan. By 1997 it had become the bestselling car in the world and by the time of its replacement by the Toyota Yaris in 2007, 35 million Toyotas had been sold.

So on average over 40 years a Corolla was sold somewhere in the world every 40 seconds.

And, in case you were wondering, Corolla is Latin for 'small crown'.

I know a lot about cars, man. I can look at any car's headlights and tell you exactly which way it's coming.

Mitch Hedberg

The lead car is unique, except for the one behind it which is identical.

Murray Walker

Traditional Late
20th Century Skoda Jokes

Q: What information do you get in every Skoda log book?
A: A bus timetable.

Q: What's the difference between a Skoda and a sheep?
A: It's a little bit less embarrassing if anyone sees you getting out of the back of a sheep.

Q: What's the difference between a Skoda and a golf ball?
A: It's usually possible to drive a golf ball more than 200 yards.

Q: Why do Skodas have heated rear windows?
A: So your hands won't get cold when you're pushing it.

Q: How do you make a Skoda completely disappear?
A: Apply rust remover.

Q: How do you get a Skoda to go 70 miles per hour?
A: Push it off Beachy Head.

Q: How do you double the value of a Skoda?
A: Fill it with petrol.

Q: What do you call a Skoda with a sun roof?
A: A skip.

Q: What do you call a Skoda with twin exhausts?
A: A wheelbarrow.

Q: What's the difference between a Skoda and a tampon?
A: The tampon comes with its own tow rope.

Q: How do you overtake a Skoda?
A: Walk a bit quicker.

Q: What do you call a Skoda with a seatbelt?
A: A rucksack.

Q: How do you get a Skoda to win a race against a Ferrari?
A: Push the Skoda off Beachy Head first.

But don't forget that by 2004 Skoda had been placed second in a survey of the best cars on British roads. So please feel free to insert the name of the car manufacturer of your choice in place of Skoda in the above jokes.

ABSOLUTE BEGINNERS!

I can't swim. I can't drive, either. I was going to learn to drive but
then I thought, well, what if I crash into a lake?

Dylan Moran

One Thing At A Time

Jane is taking her first driving lesson. Her instructor tells her,
'Now madam, this is the gear lever, down there are the pedals,
that's the clutch on the left, the brake in the middle and the
accelerator on the right...' 'Hang on a minute!' interrupts Jane.
'Let's just take one thing at a time! Teach me to drive first!'

Unhelpful Advice

You know what it's like when you try to learn anything –
everyone wants to give you advice. Which might be OK if they
weren't all telling you different things. But the worst thing is that
when you're learning and taking your test you're driving in a
way that no one else on the road does. You've seen those driving
school cars pootling along cautiously at fifteen miles an hour
while everyone behind them builds up a head of steam and starts
overtaking on the wrong side of the road just to get past. It's a
bit like being taught etiquette in preparation for your first rugby
match. You ain't gonna survive out there!

So here is some more realistic advice for learner drivers.

1. It's every man (and woman) for himself (or herself) out there.
2. Patience may be a virtue in any other walk of life but it ain't going to get you from a side road into a main road in rush hour. Go for it!
3. Don't argue with buses. They're bigger than you and you're going to come off worst.
4. Ditto articulated lorries. In spades.
5. The reason everyone drives so fast on motorways is because they want to get off as quickly as possible before they have an accident.
6. Red traffic lights mean stop, green traffic lights mean go and amber traffic lights mean whatever you want them to mean (e.g. prepare to stop if you're an old lady, or accelerate if you're a boy racer)
7. Pedestrians do not read the Highway Code. Always expect the unexpected.
8. Ditto cyclists. In spades.
9. No one knows the rules of box junctions, or if they do they're not taking much notice of them.
10. When in doubt copy what the car in front does.
11. Know where the speed cameras are. That way you're prepared when everyone in front of you suddenly jams on the brakes.
12. Don't believe a word your sat nav tells you.
13. Everyone was a learner once, but that doesn't mean you'll get any sympathy whatsoever.
14. The more easily you find somewhere to park the less likely it is that you'll be allowed to park there.
15. A car is a hole surrounded by metal into which you pour your money.

You never really learn to swear until you learn to drive.

Anon

Driving Their Parents
Round The Bend

Some people think that 17 is a bit young to be driving. Certainly the insurance companies do. If you're lucky enough to be able to afford a nice sports car at the age of seventeen you may not be able to afford the insurance as well. And we haven't even mentioned what your parents might think about you tootling off down the motorway when just a short decade ago you were tootling off down the pavement on a homemade go-cart made of a plank of wood and some old pram wheels.

In fact, the minimum driving age in the UK is actually lower than many other countries around the world. The most common age seems to be 18. Though in some places you can get behind the steering wheel at the worryingly young age of just fourteen.

In the states of both Alaska and Arkansas USA you can get a provisional driving licence at the age of fourteen, while in Montana you have to have reached the grand old age of fourteen years and six months. In Michigan you have to have got to the venerable age of fourteen years and nine months, while in New Jersey you're not allowed a provisional licence until you're virtually a geriatric at seventeen.

Quite how this all works if you're planning a coast to coast trip to celebrate your fourteenth birthday has not been explained. Presumably you have to hole up in certain states for a few months until you're old enough to move on to the next one.

While the various states of the USA have these differing ages for learner drivers there is one country where there is no such pussyfooting around. In Ethiopa anyone can drive at the age of fourteen. Though it should be noted that according to the World Health Organisation Ethiopia has the highest car accident rate in the world.

While the UK has a minimum driving age of seventeen, in the Isle of Man, just down the road as it were, you only need to be sixteen to get behind the wheel. Which would be all right, except, that the Isle of Man is the only place in the world with *no general speeding limit*. Think about it. You go to the Isle of Man for your holiday and you are driving your hire car down the road at 100 mph when you're passed by someone doing 140 who still has acne! It's enough even to give Jeremy Clarkson nightmares.

A suburban mother's role is to deliver children obstetrically once, and by car forever after.

Peter De Vries

Learning With Mum And Dad

Is learning with mum and dad really such a good idea? Let's face it, you don't listen to anything else they tell you, so why should you suddenly start listening when they say 'Whatever you do don't put diesel in it.' Or 'Brake for goodness sake!' or 'Mind that old lady!'

It's been estimated that people need roughly one or two driving lessons for every year of their life. Does this mean that a one-year-old would only need a couple of lessons at most before being fit to drive? Let's hope not.

They also say that if you learn with mum and dad you're likely to pick up their bad habits too. Such as picking your nose at traffic lights? Well maybe, but it could be even worse than that. Crossing your hands while turning the steering wheel, failing to indicate when turning, shouting abuse at other drivers, taking calls on your mobile phone...

And, depending on how old your mum and dad are, you might even find that what got them through their driving test may not be considered best practice now. Like what? Well, you don't need to change down through the gears now – e.g. going through them one by one. You can just do block gear changing which means changing straight from say fourth to second. Though perhaps not fifth to reverse.

Just The Way Dad Drives

Tom is driving along a busy road with his friend Dick when they approach a red traffic light. Tom simply speeds straight through the lights without batting an eyelid. 'What the hell are you doing?' squeals Dick. 'You've just driven straight through a red light!' 'Don't worry!' says Tom. 'I'm just doing what my dad told me to do when he taught me to drive.' When they reach another red light again Tom speeds straight through. 'You're going to get us killed!' says Dick. 'Stop worrying!' says Tom. 'I told you it's the way my dad drives.' Eventually they come to a green light and Tom slams on his brakes, making Dick bump his head on the windscreen. 'Now what are you doing?' asks Dick. 'The light's on green this time!' 'I know,' says Tom. 'And my dad might be coming from the other direction.'

I'm trying very hard to understand this generation. They have adjusted the timetable for childbearing so that menopause and teaching a sixteen-year-old how to drive a car will occur in the same week.

Erma Bombeck

Nervous Teenager

A nervous teenager is on her first driving lesson and brings her mum and dad along for moral support. Her instructor is also new to the job. As the teenager is pulling out of the car park at the beginning of her lesson, the instructor tells her, 'Turn left here, and don't forget to let the people behind know what you're doing.' The teenager turns to her parents sitting in the back seat and tells them, 'I'm going left!'

The Borrowers

Lucy has just passed her driving test and is allowed to borrow dad's car for the first time. Before she goes out, he insists that she must not be late home as she has no experience of night driving.

Of course, she goes to a party at a friend's house, rolls in at about six in the morning, and sneaks up to bed without waking her parents.

The next morning over breakfast, her father confronts her.

'OK, Lucy, what time did you get in last night?'

'Er, I can't remember exactly, Dad, but it wasn't all that late.'

'I see,' says Dad. 'In that case I'd better have a word with the newsagent about the paper boy.'

'Why?' asks Lucy, mystified.

'He's managed to wedge the paper right under the front wheel of the car!'

Dim Indicator

Kevin has bought an old banger in which to learn to drive. Before he takes it out on the road his father insists that they give it a thorough check over as he knows that his son isn't the brightest spark in the plug. They check the lights, the brakes, the steering, everything. Finally, Dad says they should check that the indicators are working properly.

'All right, Kevin,' says Dad, 'I want you to go round to the back of the car and I'll sit in the driving seat and try the indicators. Just shout out if they're working or not.'

'OK,' says Kevin, walking round to the back. 'I'm ready!'

His father tries the right indicator first. He then hears young Kevin shout out from the back:

'It's working, Dad! No, it's stopped. Oh no, it's working again. Now it's stopped again...'

ACCIDENTS WILL HAPPEN

Excuses Given By Drivers
In Car Accident Insurance Claims

I didn't think the speed limit applied after midnight.

I did not think the train ran on those lines any more.

I didn't see the lamp post.

I forgot I was in a car park.

I sneezed.

I didn't know my foot was still on the accelerator.

A lamppost bumped into my car, damaging it in two places.

It was safe when I started to make my u-turn.

I looked and there was no one close to me.

I had to take too many mobile phone calls.

I was picking my mobile phone up from the floor of the car.

How could I have known there were metal railings behind the hedge (excuse given by a driver who had reversed through someone's shrubbery).

The World's First Car Accidents

In Ireland in 1869 scientist Mary Ward fell from a steam powered automobile and was run over and killed by it.

In 1896 Mrs Bridget Driscoll was happily sauntering in the grounds of the Crystal Palace when she was mown down by Arthur Edsell, a hot-headed idiot racing along at speeds of up to 4 mph in his Roger-Benz motor car.

The following year the world's first car crash took place in London's Charing Cross Road, and the first person convicted of drink-driving was London cab driver George Smith.

A fatal accident occurred on February 25, 1899 on Grove Hill in Harrow On The Hill near London. The car in question was a Daimler Wagonette driven by a Mr Sewell who was demonstrating the vehicle to Major James Richer. Major Richer was Department Head at the Army & Navy Stores and was considering purchasing the car for the company. Mr Sewell was killed on the spot so becoming the first driver of a petrol-driven car to die in an accident. Major Richer died four days later without regaining consciousness so becoming Britain's first passenger fatality. A plaque commemorating the event was unveiled in February 1969.

The Next Best Thing
To The Brakes Working...

Dave and Alfie are out driving in Dave's ancient car. As they are heading down a steep hill, the brakes fail. Dave presses the pedal down as hard as he can, but the car keeps going faster. Alfie tries to yank the hand brake, but it comes off in his hand. 'What can we do?' he shouts. 'How can we stop this thing?' Dave shouts back, 'Brace yourself and let's try to crash into something cheap!'

The World's First Traffic Lights

Of course it may have been possible that traffic lights could have helped prevent some of the early accidents, but to begin with, there was only one set of traffic lights in the whole of London. On December 10 1868 the first set of traffic lights was installed at the corner of New Palace Yard and Bridge Street, Westminster. Consisting of red and green manually operated gas lamps the lights were put there mainly for the benefit of MPs going in and out of Parliament. They weren't greatly loved however, and this first instance of traffic lights was not repeated elsewhere. It was not until 1927 that automatic traffic lights were first used in Great Britain when they were installed in Wolverhampton at the Princes Square crossroads. America had had them in Cleveland, Ohio since 1914.

Accidents On British Roads

When the first edition of the *Highway Code* came out in 1931 there were 2.3 million motorised vehicles on Britain's roads and about 7,000 people were killed every year. Today there are over 31,000,000 vehicles on the road, but in 2008 just 2,538 people were killed on the road. In other words, just over a third of the 1931 deaths, but with over thirteen times the number of vehicles on the road. And in recent times the number of road deaths has been falling year on year. In 2006 it was 3,172, in 2007 it was 2,946, and in 2008 2,538, which, extraordinarily, was the lowest since records began in 1926.

Children in back seats cause accidents.
Accidents in back seats cause children.

Marine Car Insurance

In 1901 Lloyd's issued the first car accident injury claim motor insurance policy. A marine policy was used to provide coverage. Cars were such a novelty an underwriter wrote a normal marine policy for the car on the basis that it was a ship navigating on dry land.

Non-Safety Glass

In 1903 car windscreens were introduced. Unfortunately at first they were made from ordinary glass and thus if an accident occurred they caused horrific injuries. Safety glass was introduced in 1926 and made compulsory in 1937.

Relaxing After An Accident

Two men get out of their cars after a collision on the road. One of the men takes out a hip flask and offers it the other. 'Here! Have a sip of this,' he says. 'It might help calm your nerves.' 'Thanks,' says the other driver taking a long pull from the container before adding, 'aren't you going to have some as well?' 'No, I better not,' says the first driver. 'Well, at least not until after the police have been here.'

A Call From The Wife

John is used to getting regular calls from his wife, Jill, every time their unreliable old car breaks down. One day he gets yet another of those calls. 'What's happened this time?' he asks. 'The brakes failed,' says Jill. 'Can you come and get me?' 'OK,' says John. 'Where are you?' 'At the moment I'm in the chemist,' says Jill. 'OK,' says John, 'and where's the car?' 'It's in here with me as well,' says Jill.

The Worst Crashes Ever

Some of the worst pile-ups ever have been on motorways and are often partly due to adverse weather conditions. The combination of speed, large numbers of vehicles and poor visibility or hazardous road surfaces can be a lethal combination.

One of the worst ever motorway crashes was on the road between Dubai and Abu Dhabi on March 11, 2008. 227 cars and twelve buses were involved in a pile-up during dense fog. Ninety-two vehicles caught fire, eight people died and thirty-nine were injured.

On July 19, 2009 there was a multi-vehicle pile up in Germany on the A2 motorway. This involved 259 vehicles, and although 66 people were injured, remarkably, no one died.

Would You Get In A Car With This Man?

W.R. 'Rusty' Haight's website proudly tells the world that he has been involved in 1,000 crashes. This is because Mr Haight is Director of the Collision Safety Institute, a crash research, training and consulting centre. His job description has been given as 'traffic-collision reconstructionist'. That's human crash test dummy to me and you.

———

Researchers at an Austrian university are facing ethics charges for using human corpses as crash test dummies. See, that's what happens if you don't have a good Social Security system – you have to keep working even after you're dead.

Jay Leno

———

Did you know: Rally drivers have to display their blood group on their helmet or overalls.

Just What You Want To Hear

A man gets home from work and his wife tells him she has good news and bad news about their car. 'OK,' says the man, 'tell me the good news first.' 'Well,' says his wife, 'the air bag works...'

Remember: A tree never hit an automobile except in self defence.

Q: What part of a car causes the most accidents?
A: The nut that holds the wheel.

The Car Music Project

Have you ever drummed your fingers on the dashboard while waiting at traffic lights, joined in the concerto for massed car horns that enlivens many a European car journey, or simply whistled or sang as you drove along?

Yes, when we get into our cars we all turn into amateur musicians of some sort, but one man has gone one better. American composer Bill Milbrodt has attempted to 'turn a car into music that can be expressed in a written form.'

You've probably seen those Ford Focus TV ads where people are playing instruments made out of car parts. Well, believe it or not, they're for real!

As far back as 1995 Milbrodt had the idea of dismantling his car and turning the parts into musical instruments. He got metal sculptor Ray Faunce III to produce such instruments as 'tube flutes', 'exhaustophones' and 'fender bass' (geddit?)
Since 2005 there has been a proper band, known as 'The Car Music Project' which has played various concerts around the USA. Though it has not yet been revealed whether their tour bus is made out of musical instruments.

More Excuses From Car Accident Insurance Claims

Windscreen broken. Cause unknown. Probably voodoo.

I had been driving for 40 years when I fell asleep at the wheel and had an accident.

I told the police that I was not injured, but on removing my hat found that I had a fractured skull.

The telephone pole was approaching. I was attempting to swerve out of the way when I struck the front end.

I was on my way to the doctor with rear end trouble when my universal joint gave way causing me to have an accident.

The gentleman behind me struck me on the backside. He then went to rest in a bush with just his rear end showing.

I pulled into a lay-by because there was smoke coming from under the bonnet. I realised the car was on fire so I got my dog out and smothered it with a blanket.

I saw her look at me twice. She appeared to be making slow progress when we met on impact.

I ran into a shop window, and sustained injuries to my wife.

I misjudged a lady crossing the street.

I left my car unattended for a minute, when by accident or design, it ran away.

There were plenty of lookers-on but no witnesses.

She suddenly saw me, lost her head and we met.

Tom has found a way to make his wife drive more carefully. He told her that if she was ever in an accident the newspapers would print her real age.

Dangerous Driving

A man is driving down the motorway in a Rolls Royce convertible when a battered old van swerves at him. He manages to avoid it and the van driver does it again. As they drive along he keeps on swerving in front of the Roller, but the driver just manages to keep control of the car. Further along the motorway there is a tailback and the two vehicles end up side by side in the queue.

The Rolls Royce driver jumps out of his car and bangs on the van driver's window.

'Hey, you idiot!' he shouts. 'What were you trying to do back there? Cause an accident!?'

'Yes. I was actually,' says the man. 'You see I've just passed my test and I heard that if you had an accident with someone you have got to swap addresses.'

'So?' says the Rolls Royce driver.

'Well I'm up for that! I live in a right dump!'

Promotion Sickness

A man is driving along the road when he gets a phone call from his boss who tells him that he's been promoted. He's so excited he actually swerves the car and almost has a collision with another vehicle.

A few miles down the road the boss phones again to say that someone in the management team has just resigned so he's been promoted again. The man almost jumps out of the driving seat and swerves again.

A bit further on the phone rings again and the man is in such a state of heightened anticipation that it might be the boss promoting him again he swerves the car and crashes into a wall.

A policeman stops and asks him what happened.

'Officer, I just careered off the road.'

My new car came with an airbag with the instructions printed on it: 'In case of accident, start blowing.'

It Was The Car's Fault:
Yet More Excuses
From Accident Claims Forms

I had been learning to drive with power steering. I turned the wheel to what I thought was enough and found myself in a different direction going the opposite way.

The car in front had better brakes so I was unable to compete with the stopping distance and ended up hitting it.

I was so impressed with the car's reversing siren, I backed into a wall while listening to it.

The car didn't come with an instruction manual.

I blew my horn, but it would not work as it had been stolen.

I thought the side window was down but it was up as I found out when I put my head through it.

I don't like to hit my brakes that hard.

It Doesn't Matter
How Big Your Car Aerial Is!

If you are inside your car when it is hit by lightning, you should be completely safe – theoretically!

This is because of the Faraday Effect discovered by Michael Faraday in 1845. Faraday was Fullerian Professor of Chemistry at the Royal Institution and it is largely thanks to his work that it became viable for us to use electricity.

According to the Faraday Effect the electricity in a lightning strike will dissipate around a metal frame such as a car leaving any people inside unharmed. Electrons tend to push away from one another. When the electrons in a bolt of lightning hit your car, they will therefore run around the outside of the vehicle's metal frame in their attempt to get away from each other. The electrical power of the strike should not get inside the car.

Which is good news, apart from one thing!

These days cars aren't entirely made of metal and this might cause the Faraday Effect to be slightly less effective. There may also be some inner components that connect with the metal frame in exactly the right way to deliver the shock directly to anyone who touches them at the wrong moment. Safety advisers therefore advise that if you find yourself out in your car during a lightning storm, you should sit with your hands in your lap and avoid touching any of the car's components such as the steering wheel. Obviously this could be quite dangerous if you happen to be driving at speed at the time so it might be best to stop the car first.

In practical cases of vehicles being hit by lightning all four tyres have been blown out, car wiring systems have been damaged or destroyed and police officers who were using their radios at the time of the strike have suffered burns to their hands and mouths. So overall you should be OK... but you might not!

There Was Literally Nothing I Could Do!: Even More Excuses From Accident Claims Forms

There were too many mini roundabouts in the road and I drove into the back of the car on the one that shouldn't have been there.

I was going the wrong way down a one way street when I hit a car which was not there when going the other way.

Coming home I drove into the wrong house and collided with a tree I don't have.

As I approached an intersection a sign suddenly appeared in a place where no stop sign had ever appeared before.

My car was legally parked as it backed into another vehicle.

I pulled away from the side of the road, glanced at my mother-in-law and headed over the embankment.

I had been shopping for plants all day and was on my way home. As I reached an intersection a hedge sprang up obscuring my vision and I did not see the other car.

I was going at about 70 or 80 mph when my girlfriend on the pillion reached over and grabbed my testicles so I lost control.

When I saw I could not avoid a collision I stepped on the gas and crashed into the other car.

The accident happened when the right front door of a car came round the corner without giving a signal.

The accident occurred when I was attempting to bring my car out of a skid by steering it into the other vehicle.

CARS OF THE STARS

If you want to emulate your favourite movie/rock/rap star/
supermodel these are the cars you need to drive (start saving now):

Britney Spears – Mercedes SLR McLaren and a CLK.

Madonna – Maybach 57.

Simon Cowell – Bugatti Veyron.

Brangelina – BMW Hydrogen 7.

Jennifer Lopez – Aston Martin DB7.

Pierce Brosnan – Aston Martin Vanquish.

Janet Jackson – Aston Martin Vanquish.

Amy Winehouse – BMW 7 Series.

Paris Hilton – Mercedes Benz SLR and Bentley Continental GT.

Anna Kornikova – Cadillac Escalade EXT.

George Clooney – two seater electric Tango 600.

50 Cent – Rolls Royce Phantom.

Charlize Theron – Range Rover.

Tom Cruise – Porsche 911.

Jessica Simpson – white Escalade.

Julia Roberts – Toyota Prius (the car of choice for the
environmentally aware megastar).

Kevin Costner – Audi Q7 and Audi S8.

Lindsay Lohan – Mercedes SL65 AMG.

Nicole Richie and Joel Madden – Bentley Continental.

Jerry Seinfeld – Porsche.

Samuel Jackson – Maybach 57 S.

George W. Bush – Cadillac DTS limousine.

Leonardo DiCaprio – Toyota Prius.

Colin Farrell – black Ford Bronco.

Kirsten Dunst – Toyota Prius.

Justin Timberlake – white Jeep Wrangler Unlimited.

Kate Moss – vintage MG.

Ice-T – red Bentley convertible.

Missy Elliott – Aston Martin V12 Vanquish, Rolls Royce Phantom and Lamborghini Gallardo.

David Beckham – Cadillac Escalade.

Jim Carrey – Mercedes S-Class.

Wyclef Jean – $350,000 Pagani Zonda C12-S, a Ferrari 360 Spyder, an F1 McLaren and a Mercedes G-500 (though not all at once presumably).

Fergie – H2.

Tyra Banks – Lexus SC.

Matthew Perry – Porsche convertible.

Sienna Miller – Audi TT.

Cars Of The Screen

Have you ever watched a film where the cars are more interesting than the actors? The acting may be wooden, but at least the cars are steel and chrome. Over the years many films and TV series have benefited hugely from the sudden appearance of a fabulous motor, and some car chases have become the stuff of Hollywood legend. And just once in a while a car achieves a fame and a celebrity all of its own. Would the 1960s TV series of *Batman* been half as exciting if Batman and Robin had raced away from the Batcave in a Honda Civic? Would the travels of Inspector Morse through green and lush Oxfordshire countryside have been half as appealing if he'd been sitting behind the wheel of a Ford Ka? And would Steve McQueen's car chase in *Bullitt* have hit the spot if he'd had his foot to the floor in a Reliant Robin?
So, lest we forget, here are some of the most iconic four-wheeled stars of film and TV:

The Batmobile

The Batmobile was in fact, a Lincoln Futura concept car. In other words, it was a one-off. When the TV show was looking for a car for the start of the 1966 series they asked Hollywood car customising expert George Barris to get to work. Luckily, he happened to have a car handy that he could adapt. The vehicle had already starred in the 1959 Debbie Reynolds film *It Started With a Kiss*, though by the time he'd finished with it three weeks later it was more suited to our Caped Crusader than the leading lady in a 1950s rom com. Though some of the elements, such as the hooded headlight pods and the exaggerated futuristic tailfins were already in place before the customisation began. George Barris bought the car from Ford in 1965 for a nominal $1, and by 2009 it was believed to be worth around two million times that amount! There are also three copies of the Batmobile in existence; two made for exhibition purposes, and a third built for the drag-racing circuit. There have of course been other versions of the Batmobile in comics going back to the very first Batman story in *Detective Comics* 27, and others in various film versions, but for many people the sight of the rocket-launched 1960s TV Batmobile speeding from the Batcave will be the definitive one.

The Love Bug

Also known as Herbie, and star of no less than five different cinema films as well as a made for TV film, and a TV series. Herbie is one of only two cars ever to feature in the cast credits at the end of a film (the other one is Eleanor from *Gone in 60 Seconds*). It is said that when casting took place for the film other cars had to 'audition' for the part, including Toyotas, Volvos and an MG. The number 53 emblazoned on Herbie is taken from the number on the shirt of LA Dodgers baseball star Don Drysdale, a detail which had been suggested by the film's producer, who was a fan.

Herbie was of course a Volkswagen Beetle, though up until just before the film was released in 1968 that model of car was still officially known as a Volkswagen type 1. 'Beetle' was simply a nickname given due to its distinctive shape. Volkswagen didn't officially start advertising the car in the USA as a Beetle until August 1967. Could this have been anything to do with the popularity of a certain Liverpudlian band of that era one wonders?

The idea for the Volkswagen ('people's car' in German) was famously first put forward by Adolf Hitler. So, from Hitler to Herbie in 35 years – who'd have thought it?

The *Back to the Future* car

When Marty McFly goes back in time from 1985 to 1955 he doesn't use just any old time machine, he uses a De Lorean DMC-12 which has been especially adapted by his professor friend Dr. Emmett 'Doc' Brown. The DMC-12 was of course a real car, manufactured by the DeLorean Motor Company. Despite being a left-hand drive car made for the American market the DMC-12 was manufactured in Northern Ireland. Over 9000 DMCs were produced between 1981 and 1982, but only seventeen right-hand drive models were produced.

With its distinctive 'gull-wing' doors the DeLorean DMC-12 was the perfect car for the part in Back to the Future – at once retro and futuristic. When the right-hand drive models rolled off the production line the top speed shown on some of the speedometers was 140 mph, but the top speed on the left-hand drive models was just 85 mph. Tricky for Marty McFly and 'Doc' Brown, as according to his theory of time travel the DeLorean needed to reach a speed of 88 mph.

So, if you're lucky enough to own a DeLorean DMC-12 do you need to keep your speed under 88 mph to avoid not just the traffic cops but also inadvertent travel through time? Not unless you just happen to have the necessary plutonium on board to create a nuclear reaction. Drive safely now!

James Bond's Aston Martin DB5

In the book Goldfinger, 007 was driving a DB Mark III but by the time the film came out in 1964 this had been superseded by the DB4, and the prototype of the DB5 was newly ready. This prototype was used in the film (though they did have a standard car for stunts). It now had a 3995cc engine (as opposed to the Mark III's 2.9L one) and had a top speed of 145 mph. Bond's car naturally had a couple of little extras such as the gun barrels that popped out from behind the front indicators and a bullet-proof shield behind the rear window.

The DB5 also made appearances in the films Thunderball, Golden Eye, Tomorrow Never Dies and Casino Royale. Only just over a thousand DB5s were made and if you had bought one back in 1964 it would have set you back £4,248, or about £1,000 more than the price of an average house in the UK.

And what did the DB stand for? The slightly disappointing answer is David Brown, who was the head of Aston Martin from 1947 to 1972.

Bond's Cars

James Bond's car of choice in many of Ian Fleming's novels is a battleship grey 1933 Bentley convertible with a 4.5 litre engine coupled with an Amherst Villiers supercharger.

In the films, Bond however has been noticeably more promiscuous in his motoring habits, having driven the following over the past few decades:

Sean Connery:
Dr No (1962) – 1961 Sunbeam Alpine Series II

From Russia With Love (1963) – Bentley 4½ Litre Sports Tourer

Goldfinger (1964) – Aston Martin DB5

Thunderball (1965) – Aston Martin DB5

George Lazenby:
On Her Majesty's Secret Service (1969) – Aston Martin DB5

Sean Connery:
Diamonds Are Forever (1971) – Ford Mustang Mach 1

Roger Moore:
Live and Let Die (1973) – Coronado

The Man With The Golden Gun (1974) – AMC Hornet hatchback special coupe

The Spy Who Loved Me (1977) – Lotus Esprit S1

Moonraker (1979) – MP Roadster

For Your Eyes Only (1981) – Lotus Esprit Turbo

Octopussy (1983) – Mercedes 250 SE, black & Alfa Romeo GTV

A View to a Kill (1985) – Renault 11 taxis

Timothy Dalton:
The Living Daylights (1987) – Aston Martin DBS V8 Vantage & Volante & Audi 200 Quattro

Licence to Kill (1989) – Lincoln Mark VII LSC

Pierce Brosnan:
Goldeneye (1995) – Aston Martin DB5 & BMW Z3 roadster

Tomorrow Never Dies (1997) – BMW 750iL & Aston Martin DB5

The World Is Not Enough (1999) – BMW Z8

Die Another Day (2002) – Aston Martin V12 Vanquish

Daniel Craig:
Casino Royale (2006) – Aston Martin DBS V12

Quantum of Solace (2008) – Aston Martin DBS V12

As Much Use As
A Chocolate Racing Car!

A team from the University of Warwick developed the world's first formula 1 racing car to run on and to be made from sustainable, renewable materials:

According to Dr Kerry Kirwan from the research team:

'Components made from plants form the mainstay of the car's make up, including a race specification steering wheel derived from carrots and other root vegetables, a flax fibre and soybean oil foam racing seat, a woven flax fibre bib, plant oil based lubricants and a bio-diesel engine configured to run on fuel derived from waste chocolate and vegetable oil. It also incorporates a radiator coated in a ground-breaking emission destroying catalyst.'

So if the car crashes presumably you can just mash it up and make it into soup.

Nevertheless the car is still capable of taking corners at 125 mph. Not only that, but the vehicle cleans the air as it drives thanks to that revolutionary emission destroying catalyst.

There is however apparently no truth in the rumour that the inventor of the root vegetable, soy bean and chocolate car was once the owner of an unsuccessful whole-food restaurant.

Fill Her Up With Five Gallons Of Uranium

The Model T, the Thunderbird, the Zodiac, the Prefect, the Cortina, the Escort, the Focus.

The Ford Motor Company has successfully marketed many vehicles over the years. But there was also one which definitely didn't catch on so well.

Designed in 1957 the Ford Nucleon resembled a shiny 1950s style space ship. The car also dispensed with the normal internal combustion engine in favour of the exciting new power source of the moment. Yes, the Ford Nucleon would have been the world's first atomic powered runabout. It was the car with its own nuclear fission reactor in the boot. What could possibly go wrong!

It was anticipated that the Nucleon would be able to travel for 5,000 miles before it needed re-charging. It would also be comparatively very quiet. Unless of course you happened to accidentally reverse into a concrete post which would send a mushroom cloud several miles up into the atmosphere.

The smallest reactor available is however that used in nuclear submarines. At the time of the Nucleon's design it was assumed that smaller nuclear reactors and lighter shielding materials would soon be developed. Unfortunately though, they weren't. And even though the passenger compartment was situated well away from the reactor, for many it would not have seemed quite far enough!

The car would however have got round the problem people often have of not wanting a nuclear reactor in their backyard. The Ford Nucleon would have given them one in their front driveway instead.

And of course if you were driving one, other drivers might be particularly careful not to rear end you. Particularly when they read your 'Nuclear Reactor on board' bumper sticker!

The Dymaxion

American inventor, designer, author and futurist, Richard Buckminster 'Bucky' Fuller (1895–1983) not only popularised the geodesic dome, he also came up with one of the world's weirdest ever cars.

The Dymaxion was part of Fuller's general project to make the world a better place for humanity. It was a 20 foot long, teardrop shaped, three wheeler, mini-van capable of doing a U-turn in its own length. It could carry 11 people, do 30 miles per gallon and travel at 120 mph. And this was in 1933!

It was also intended that the Dymaxion would fly jump-jet style as soon as suitable alloys and engines became available.

The vehicle was demonstrated at the 1933 Chicago World's Fair. Tragically the demonstration ended in an accident which killed the driver and injured its passengers. The Dymaxion never went into production.

The Car That Doubles As
A Pull-Along Vacuum Cleaner!

Clive Sinclair was the inventor of the slim-line pocket calculator and the man who gave Britain its first mass market home computer. He then followed up this incredible series of innovations with a revolutionary new form of motor transport: the Sinclair C5.

The C5 was a one-seater tricycle powered by an electric battery and which was capable of doing a top speed of 15 mph. It was also possible to pedal the vehicle if the battery ran out of power. In practice it proved necessary to pedal quite a lot of the time. It retailed at £399 plus another £143 if you wanted all the accessories such as wing mirrors and indicators that were felt necessary to make the vehicle safe to drive.

The C5 had a body designed with the help of the Lotus sports car company no less! It had been created to take advantage of a change in the law in 1983 which meant that it could be driven without insurance, driving licence, road tax or crash helmet by anyone over the age of 14. Despite this, hardly anyone over the age of 14 wanted to drive one.

The C5 was launched in January 1985. This proved to be an inauspicious time to launch a vehicle in which the driver was completely exposed to the elements and the battery suffered severe loss of power as a result of damp and cold temperatures.

The end of production was announced eight months after the launch. Two months later Sinclair Vehicles had gone into receivership. Just 12,000 C5s had been sold. In subsequent years it became a collectors' item and one could now set you back as much as £1,000.

The World's Most Expensive Car

Just in case you win the lottery some time soon, you may well be thinking of what car you could possibly buy to reflect your new-found wealth.

Probably the priciest new car on the market today is the Bugatti Veyron, which at £1,200,000 would make a bit of a dent in your lottery win. Not only that you've got to be able to keep it in petrol. When this car gets to its top speed of around 250 mph it's getting through about two gallons a minute, which would empty the tank in just twelve minutes. But hey, you've just won the lottery, you can afford it!

If your lottery win doesn't turn out to be quite enough for a Bugatti Veyron then you could always plump for the Lamborghini Reventon, a snip at around £986,000. The only problem is that Lamborghini are rumoured to be making only twenty of these little beauts, and they're all spoken for.

Around the same price is the Aston Martin One-77, so called because only seventy-seven of them will be made.

Of course all the above prices are for new cars. If you want to buy a classic old car you may have to win a rollover. A bog standard lottery win may just not be quite enough – especially if you're thinking of buying petrol as well.

In 1987 a 1931 Bugatti Royal Kellner sold for a whopping £5,500,000, and in 2008 DJ Chris Evans paid £5,089,280 for a black Ferrari 250 GT California Spyder that once belong to actor James Coburn.

But the record price for a car was the £15,700,000 paid at auction in 2008 for a Ferrari GTO. Only thirty-nine of these were built between 1962 and 1964. The British buyer remained anonymous. Perhaps he didn't want the wife to find out!

TALES OF MR TOWED

One Of The Most Depressing Moments In Life

There are few more depressing moment in your life, if you are an enthusiastic owner-driver, than when you are forced to admit that your car is no longer in its prime.

Practical Car Owner Illustrated, 1955

You Could Break Down In Tears

Yes, it's the nightmare scenario. You're just off on holiday, you've got the car packed to the gills with luggage, buckets, spades, and dinghies and maybe even some kids, then half down the motorway your trusty old motor gives up the ghost.
It has been estimated that the average driver experiences a break down 20 times over his or her driving life. Considering that some people change their car almost as often as their socks and probably never suffer anything so inconvenient darling, that probably means that Joe and Joanna Soap are probably going to have to put up with this inconvenience even more often than that. And it does always happen at the absolute worst time doesn't it? You're on your way to a wedding, or a funeral; it happens in the middle of Bulgaria; it's in the ASBO capital of Britain – at night; it's when you're on your way to the most important job interview of your life. It's at times like this that you sympathise totally with Basil Fawlty in that famous scene where he gave his car a 'damn good thrashing.'

I want a pit crew... I hate the procedure I currently have to go through when I have car problems.

Dave Barry

———

Over the years Tom's car has been up and down on the garage lift so often he thinks it must be the only vehicle that has done a higher mileage vertically than horizontally.

———

There's nothing wrong with the car... except that it's on fire.

Murray Walker

Turning The Clock Back

Dick is trying to sell his ancient old banger. Unfortunately he is having trouble finding a buyer, because the car has 340,000 miles on the clock. One day his friend, Tom, tells him, 'There may be a way of selling that car of yours, but I'm afraid it's not going to be entirely legal.' 'That doesn't matter,' says Dick, 'as long as I am able to sell the car.' Tom gives him the address of a car mechanic. 'Tell him I sent you,' says Tom, 'and he will turn the counter on your car back so it shows just 40,000 miles. Then it shouldn't be so difficult to find a buyer.' A month later Tom and Dick run into each other again. 'Tell me,' says Tom, 'did you ever manage to sell that car of yours?' 'No,' says Dick. 'There's no need. It's only got 40,000 miles on the clock now!'

———

I had to stop driving my car for a while... the tyres got dizzy.

Steven Wright

Repair North!

In 2007 Warranty Direct conducted a survey on garage repair bills and found that the cost of a mechanic varied wildly, especially depending on which part of the country you lived in. So in Fife, Scotland for example, you could find a mechanic for £55.40 an hour, while in London the price could be as high as £183.30 an hour! So, if you break down in London you know exactly what to do – drive up to Fife and save a fortune! Oh, hang on though, your car's not working is it?

A Poor Service

In 2002 the Department of Trade and Industry (DTI) carried out an undercover investigation of 207 UK garages. Amazingly, and rather shockingly, they found that only 5% gave a very good service (no pun intended presumably). Of course it's possible that by some sheer fluke they picked the 207 worst garages in the UK, but that's probably not very likely. They estimated that sub-standard work and overcharging was costing motorists £100 billion a year! They found that 86% of garages missed at least one of the faults on the test cars while 27% did work that was unnecessary.

But hold on a minute. If only 5% were giving a very good service and 86% missed one of the faults, that means that 9% of the not very good garages were finding the faults! Let's try and big up the garages a bit here. Also, if 27% were doing work that was unnecessary could they not get some sort of franchise deal with all the garages that were missing stuff? These figures also seem to indicate that 13% of garages were missing real faults, yet at the same time inventing ones that weren't there. Imagine if doctors worked like this. Perhaps if we paid for operations they would. You could go in for an ingrowing toenail and come out missing an appendix. The answer must be therefore some sort of National Health Service for cars.

Fan Belt Repair

A young couple are driving along the road when the car suddenly conks out. The man looks under the bonnet and then leans in through the window to his wife and says, 'Oh dear, you'd better take your tights off.'

'Oh it's the fan belt is it?' says the woman, 'And you're going to use my tights to fix it until we can get to a garage.'

'No,' says the man, 'I'm going to phone the AA, but I thought we might as well amuse ourselves while we're waiting.'

Got It Taped

A young married couple are taking her mother out for the day but when they are driving along a country lane miles from anywhere the car suddenly comes to a shuddering halt. The man opens up the bonnet and has a look, then goes to the glove compartment and gets out a roll of gaffer tape.

His wife looks impressed. 'Oh, Pete,' she says, 'you're so clever with your hands. I knew you'd be able to fix it. But will that tape be strong enough?'

'It's not for the car,' says the husband, 'I just want to keep your mother quiet while we sit here for hours waiting to be towed.'

Q: What should you do if a bird craps on your car?
A: Don't take her out again.

Most Momentous Motoring Moment

In 1999 Nat West bank commissioned a poll to find the nation's 'Most Momentous Motoring Moment'. They were all there, the first Model T Ford in1909, Sir Malcolm Campbell breaking the land speed record in 1933, Damon Hill winning the F1 World Championship in 1996. Our finest hours. But top of the poll was Basil Fawlty thrashing his car with a tree branch after it refused to start on his all-important Gourmet Night. It even beat the iconic car chase from the Italian Job into second place. That's how deep in our psyche the fear of – and anger generated by – a car breakdown lies.

Dodgy Builders

A woman hires some dodgy builders to lay a new path at the front of the house. They spend a few hours doing it and charge her £800. The woman looks at it and it's all wonky and badly laid so she refuses to pay. She then walks down to the shops for some retail therapy.

When she gets back she finds the builders have smashed the windscreen of her car and have thrown all the paving slabs into it. She tries to pull them out but they are too heavy.

She is absolutely horrified and phones her husband at work in a hysterical state trying to explain what has happened.

'Look calm down love,' says the husband, 'Just explain slowly and calmly what the problem is.'

'The problem is,' she explains between sobs, 'I can't get the drive out of the car!'

The Government's Take On Breakdowns

It's always worth finding out the official figures on breakdowns if only to assure yourself that it's not just you who always gets the greasy end of the dipstick.

What better place than the DFT (Department For Transport) website? But watch out sir, there's a bit of jargon ahead. First you encounter 'delay modelling in quadro' whatever that might be, and then you get on to the 'incident delay submodel'.

Yes, if your car breaks down it's an incident delay submodel. This part of the website will tell you that the submodel assumes that breakdowns occur at the rate of 10 per 106 veh-km for light vehicles. It will also tell you that a breakdown will result in 80% of the lane you have broken down in being blocked and 15% of adjacent lanes too. Or, to put it another way, if N lanes are open past the worksite (e.g. where you're standing looking at your car and wondering how much it's going to cost this time) each with a normal capacity of C then the site capacity during a breakdown would be reduced to: C [0.2 + 0.85 (N-1)]. Handy to know eh?

The AA & Breakdowns

That's the Automobile Association by the way, for any American readers, and not Alcoholics Anonymous. According to the AA one of the most common causes of vehicle breakdown is a flat or faulty battery. One of the other most common causes is lost keys. Eh? Lost keys? How do you lose your keys while you're actually going along the road?

That's Blown It

A woman dents her car and takes it to a garage to get it fixed. The mechanics at the garage quickly realise the woman knows nothing about cars so they decide to have a bit of fun with her. 'What you have to do to get the dent out,' they tell her, 'is take the car home, lie down at the back and blow into the exhaust pipe. The air pressure will make the dent pop back out again!' So the woman takes the car home, lies down behind it and starts blowing up the exhaust pipe without any obvious success. An hour later her husband arrives home and finds her blowing into the exhaust. When he finds out what the mechanics have told her to do, he stands looking aghast. 'You stupid woman!' he tells her. 'You're never going to blow the dent out like that are you? You've left the windows open!'

There's No Fuel Like An Old Fuel

Another reason for breakdowns is drivers putting the wrong sort of fuel in the car. It's been estimated that 100,000 people a year put diesel in petrol cars or vice versa. Is that the same 100,000 people every year, or a different lot? If it's the same lot that means that we don't learn much from our mistakes. If it's a different lot, that means that a) we're not learning much from other people's mistakes, b) by about 2035 every car driver in Britain will have put the wrong fuel into their car at some point in their motoring lives.

ENGINUITY
How A Motor Car Works

All cars today use what is known as an internal combustion engine. As the name suggests, it is an engine which produces power from heat generated inside itself, as distinct from the steam engine which applies heat generated from coal or oil burnt outside itself.

Practical Car Owner Illustrated, 1955

The automobile engine will come, and then I will consider my life's work complete.

Rudolf Diesel

The Basics

Cars. We take them for granted really don't we? Gone are the days when they used to break down every five minutes, when you had to hand-crank them to get them started, or when you tried to repair them yourself. At one time it was fairly common for a bloke (and it usually was a bloke, ladies) to have a go at fixing the car when it went wrong. The only time he called in the missus was when he wanted to borrow one of her stockings to temporarily replace a broken fan belt. But now? Most people will look under the bonnet of a car and not have the foggiest idea what does what, let alone know how to fix it when it goes wrong.

The Internal Combustion Engine

Is there such a thing as an external combustion engine? Well yes, ye olde steam train burned the fuel outside the engine so it was an external combustion engine, whereas cars burn the fuel inside the engine which is much more efficient.

The first person to design an internal combustion engine was Dutch scientist Christian Huygens in 1673. Though he never actually got around to building it, which may be just as well because instead of using petrol to power it he was planning on using gunpowder. So if he had succeeded it might have brought a whole new meaning to the expression 'old banger'.

Then in 1856 a couple of Italian inventors, Felice Matteucci and Eugenio Barsanti, patented a three-stroke engine in London which failed unfortunately to bring them fame and fortune.

In fact, the question of who actually invented the internal combustion engine that we know today is... well, open to question. It has been estimated that the modern car is the end result of over 100,000 different patents. No wonder we're all mind-boggled when we look under the bonnet.

It takes 8,460 bolts to assemble an automobile, and one nut to scatter it all over the road.

Anonymous

As Any Fuel Knows

Apart from gunpowder or petrol what else can you use to fuel your car? Diesel of course, kerosene.... How about gasohol? A mixture of eight or nine parts petrol to one or two parts alcohol. It may work, but what a waste of good booze. Then you've got compressed natural gas (CNG), liquefied petroleum gas (LPG), bio ethanol, bio diesel.... Or you could go electric, or steam-driven (stop laughing at the back there).

The Four-Stroke Engine

Cars use a four-stroke engine. In the first down stroke the inlet valves to the cylinder open and the piston descends drawing a mixture of petrol and air into the cylinder.

Then with both of the inlet valves now closed, the piston comes back up to the top of the cylinder compressing the mixture.

Power is provided in the second down stroke when the piston is driven downwards by the expansion of the mixture after it has been ignition by the spark plug.

In the final up stroke the burnt gas is pushed out of the cylinder into the exhaust system as the piston comes up for the second time.

The car's cylinders are arranged on a crankshaft so that they fire at equal intervals on every two revolutions of the crankshaft so providing an even distribution of power.

Full Steam Ahead

Yes, driving a steam-powered car these days may sound comical but on August 25th 2009 the British Steam Car achieved 139.843 mph and broke the land speed record for a steam-powered vehicle. The car was driven by Charles Burnett III. The next day Don Wales hit 148.308 in the same car. Both records took place at Edwards' Air Force Base in California, USA. Surely those speeds should be enough for even the most die-hard petrol heads.

Wake Up And Smell The Biofuel!

Coffee can also be used to make fuel for your car.

Spent coffee grounds contain between 10 to 15% of oil that can be refined into biofuel. Researchers from the University of Nevada experimented using coffee grounds from Starbucks and demonstrated that 100% of the oil in the grounds could be converted into biodiesel. They estimated that $8 million profit could be made from the coffee waste of the USA alone while globally the gunk at the bottom of the world's percolators could be turned into 340 million gallons of fuel a year.

And not only will your car smell delicious, there shouldn't be any danger of falling asleep at the wheel!

———

New Scientist magazine reported that in the future, cars could be powered by hazelnuts. That's encouraging, considering an eight-ounce jar of hazelnuts costs about nine dollars. Yeah, I've got an idea for a car that runs on bald eagle heads and Faberge eggs.

Jimmy Fallon

Seriously Alternative Energy

In 2007 it was reported that AMEC were planning to build a plant in Quebec, Canada to produce biodiesel from nappies. Yes, the plastics, resins and fibres of the nappies along with their squidgy aromatic contents could all be converted into diesel using a pyrolysis process.

But what smell will your car leave as it drives past?

And will your exhaust have to be adapted so it makes an appropriate noise?

———

They think they can make fuel from horse manure – now, I don't know if your car will be able to get 30 miles to the gallon, but it's sure gonna put a stop to siphoning.

Billie Holiday

Electrickery

The electric car isn't slow off the starting blocks either. The first ever land speed record was claimed by an electric car in 1899. The Comte de Chasseloup-Laubet achieved 57.6 mph at Acheres in France. The most recent land speed record for an electric car is pretty impressive too. The Buckeye Bullet broke the US electric land speed record with a speed of 314.958 mph. Incidentally, the Buckeye Bullet 2, a hydrogen fuel cell powered vehicle set a record of over 300 mph in 2009.

Fuel Gobbler

The remains of turkey dinners can also be used to power cars. In Carthage, Missouri the pioneering alternative fuel company CWT (Changing World Technologies) opened a plant to convert turkey waste from the nearby Butterball turkey processing plant.

The plant used a process of thermal depolymerisation which is similar to the natural process which produces fossil fuels. Except it takes a few hours rather than a few million years to achieve.

Each day at CWT's Carthage plant, two hundred and seventy tons of turkey guts were used to produce 400 barrels of biodiesel. At first it was predicted that the resulting fuel would cost just $15 a barrel to produce. Unfortunately by April 2006 the actual price had turned out to be around $80. This meant that for about half the time the plant had been running, the company had been making a $40 loss on each barrel produced. By March 2009 CWT had filed for bankruptcy and the Carthage plant was effectively shut down.

And this wasn't the only problem the plant had faced. During its operation the plant local residents had repeatedly complained about its appalling smells although at one stage an investigation showed that these were not emanating from the plant!

TESTING TIMES

Driving is an art in which those who are engaged should, in the interest of their own and of the public's safety, take the greatest pains to make themselves proficient.

Leslie Hore-Belisha (UK Transport Minister, 1935)

Water-Cooled

A rich woman rushes into the drawing room of her posh country house and shouts to her husband.

'Darling! It's the car!'

'What is it my precious?' asks the husband.

'There's water in the carburettor.'

'But darling,' exclaims the husband, 'You don't know the first thing about cars! How do you know there's water in the carburettor, you soppy old thing?'

'Because I drove it into the swimming pool!'

The Birth Of The UK Driving Test

In the UK in the late 19th and early 20th centuries, there was no driving test. Instead you might receive training as part of your job or alternatively you could get a friend to teach you. Or of course there was always the option to teach yourself! No, seriously! In those days self-tuition driving lessons were a genuine option!

Learning to drive was a lot easier during this period. There wasn't too much to learn or too many rules and regulations in those halcyon early days of motoring. Unfortunately this lack of rules and regulations for driver conduct inevitably led to an extraordinary number of accidents and deaths on the road. Some might therefore say that the British government was rather slow off the mark in not introducing the Highway Code until 1931.

Driving tests had been established and examiners appointed in 1930. The first UK tests were however only for disabled drivers (of which presumably there were many in the years following the Great War). These disabled drivers were granted licences valid for a year at a time.

At last the 1934 Road Traffic Act introduced the driving test for all drivers starting from early 1935. In accordance with the UK's apparently rather relaxed attitude to driving standards at the time, the test was at first voluntary! In fact the voluntary test was offered to help avoid too much of a backlog when testing became compulsory. From 1st June 1935, all drivers who had started driving on or after 1st April 1934 had to take a driving test.

The minimum driving age of 17 and the urban speed limit of 30 mph were both set in the UK in 1930.

Another Fine Mess...

The transport minister who first introduced formal testing for drivers in 1934 was Oliver Stanley – presumably not named as a tribute to the popular Hollywood double act of the time.

First Person To Pass His Driving Test: Mr Bean!

On March 16, 1935, London resident Mr J Beene became the first person in the UK to pass his driving test. The test cost him 7 shillings and 6d (37.5 new pence). There were no test centres at the time. So Mr Beene's examiner would have made a booking with him and arranged to meet him for his test at some pre-arranged spot. Meeting places such as a car park or a railway station were suggested. Mr Beene had learnt to drive with the British School of Motoring who had been called on by the Ministry of Transport to help set up a practical driving test.

The traffic was terrible the day Archie did his driving test. In fact it was so bad that in the end his examiner told him to abandon his car and carry on the test on foot.

The French Needed To Learn To Drive First

France had been almost 40 years ahead of the UK having introduced driving tests, vehicle registration plates and parking restrictions in 1893. This was not because French drivers were completely inept compared to their British counterparts but because of an early attempt to improve road safety standards. Furthermore 35 years before the first British man to pass his test, Vera Hedges Butler had become the first British woman to get a licence. In 1900 Miss Butler had therefore had to travel to France in order to pass her test.

French Exchange

A driving instructor tells a colleague, 'I think I'm going to take that old lady I'm teaching over to France for a few days.' 'Really?' asks his shocked colleague. 'Why?' 'Well,' says the instructor, 'it might do her good to find out what it's like to drive on the wrong side of the road legally!'

The First Examiners

When compulsory testing was brought in on June 1, 1935, the UK had 250 examiners. They took between 9 to 16 half-hour driving tests each day. Two hundred and forty six thousand people applied to take their test of which 63% passed.

And Here Are
The Reasons You Failed...

According to the UK Driving Standards Agency the top
10 reasons why people fail their driving test are:

1. Observation at junctions – ineffective observation and
   judgement

2. Reverse parking – ineffective observation or a lack of
   accuracy

3. Use of mirrors – not checking or not acting on the
   information

4. Reversing around a corner – ineffective observation or a lack
   of accuracy

5. Incorrect use of signals – not cancelling, or giving misleading
   signals

6. Moving away safely – ineffective observation

7. Incorrect positioning on the road – at roundabouts or on
   bends

8. Lack of steering control – steering too early or leaving it too
   late

9. Incorrect positioning to turn right – at junctions and in one
   way streets

10. Inappropriate speed – travelling too slowly or being hesitant

The DSA calculated that those who passed their driving test had, on average, had around 45 hours of professional tuition plus 22 hours of private practice. The pass rate was 43% overall and was much lower if only first time candidates were taken into account. Each year more than 100,000 people fail their driving test in the UK.

Driving examiner: What does a yellow line mean?
Irishman: You can't park there at all.
Driving examiner: OK. And what does a double yellow line mean?
Irishman: You can't park there at all...at all.

949 Test Failures

It was reported in 2009 that a 68-year old South Korean lady called Mrs Cha had finally passed her driving test on the 950th attempt.

Congratulations, Mrs Cha! Now try and put the 949 failures out of your mind!

Mrs Cha had been taking her driving test on an almost daily basis since 13th April 2005 because, she said, she wanted a car to help with her business selling items door to door.

Nevertheless the cost of taking the test so many times was staggering. Each individual test cost 6,000 won (about £3). It was estimated that Mrs Cha had spent around 5 million won in her attempt to get herself a licence.

And of course this was just the written test! It is necessary to score 60 out of 100 to pass the Korean written driving test. Unfortunately Mrs Cha's usual score was less than 50 points.

Anyway she's at last got her written exam out of the way. Now it's just the difficult bit of the test left to do!

Driving examiner: When driving through fog, what should you use?
Learner: A car?

Splash = Crash

In September 2008 a woman failed her driving test for splashing a man standing at a bus stop. The 31-year-old was taking her test in Blackley, North Manchester when she drove through a puddle and splashed the pedestrian's shoes.

According to her examiner splashing the pedestrian constituted a crash and, as such, an instant fail. The driver should have stopped the car and exchanged insurance details with the soaking man. Exchanging a towel might have been useful as well.

Your Driving Test Has Been Postponed For The Duration Of Hostilities

Driving tests were suspended in the UK on September 2, 1939. Tests did not resume until November 1, 1946. Testing was again suspended on November 24, 1956 during the Suez Crisis. During this period of suspension, learners were allowed to drive unaccompanied and examiners helped to administer petrol rations.

Written Test Answers

The following are – allegedly – a selection of genuine answers received during examinations given by the California Department of Transportation's driving school.

Q: Who has the right of way when four cars approach a four-way stop at the same time?

A: The pick up truck with the gun rack and the bumper sticker saying, 'Guns don't kill people. I do.'

Q: What problems would you face if you were arrested for drunk driving?

A: I'd probably lose my buzz a lot faster.

Q: What changes would occur in your lifestyle if you could no longer drive lawfully?

A: I would be forced to drive unlawfully.

Q: What are some points to remember when passing or being passed?

A: Make eye contact and wave 'hello' if she is cute.

Q: What is the difference between a flashing red traffic light and a flashing yellow traffic light?

A: The colour.

Q: How do you deal with heavy traffic?

A: Heavy psychedelics.

Q: What can you do to help ease a heavy traffic problem?

A: Carry loaded weapons.

Q: Why would it be difficult to be a police officer?

A: It would be tough to be an idiot all day long.

Baby, He Can Drive His Own Car

John Lennon decided to learn to drive at Christmas 1964 and
enrolled with a driving school in Weybridge. He passed his test,
at the centre in Queens Road, Weybridge, in February 1965,
after only seven lessons. The local paper said that his instructor
described Lennon as 'one of the most apt pupils I have ever had in
my 30 years of driving instruction.'

Well known 20th century scientific genius Albert Einstein never
learned to drive a car.

I'm Going To Tap
The Dashboard Once...

Archie is taking his driving test. The examiner tells him that
when he taps the dashboard, he wants Archie to demonstrate
what action he would take if someone had just stepped out in
front of the car. The examiner taps the dashboard and Archie
demonstrates his emergency stop. 'Very good,' says the examiner.
'Now drive on.'

Archie drives on, but immediately a man steps out right in front
of the car and Archie ploughs right into him. 'What the hell do
you think you're doing!?' squeals the examiner in horror. 'It's your
fault!' Archie yells back. 'You didn't tap the dashboard that time!'

Mirror, Signal, Manoeuvre, Car Jack!

In 2003 an 18-year-old British man suffered a carjacking in the middle of taking his driving test.

The man was doing his test in Clacton on Sea in Essex. He had stopped ready to reverse around a corner when he and his examiner suddenly found themselves being dragged out of their Ford Fiesta by two men in crash helmets.

The men had just raided a nearby Post Office and had escaped with a cash box. They had however evidently forgotten to employ the services of a getaway driver to assist with the crime. In fact they had made an attempt to escape the scene on a motorbike but had been boxed in by police.

They somehow managed to squeeze their crash helmeted heads inside the Fiesta and made their escape in a car displaying L plates and the insignia of Tendring School of Motoring. The car was found abandoned 20 minutes later.

The driver and his examiner were naturally left very shaken by the incident. A police spokesman commented, 'The test is hard enough without this.'

It is understood that the examiner did not grant the carjackers a pass either.

Blind Crossing

A man is on his driving test when a blind man crosses the road in front of him. The driver carries on and nearly runs the blind man down. 'What the hell's the matter with you?' asks the driving examiner. 'Don't you know you're supposed to slow down to let blind people cross?' 'What's the point?' says the driver. 'How was he going to see my number plate?'

Ozzy Passes!

Ozzy Osbourne finally passed his driving test in October 2009 at the age of 60.

He had first taken the test in 1974 but told newspapers he couldn't remember how many times he had failed: 'I've lost count how many times. I remember one time I was doing the three-point turn and I passed out because I'd been to the doctor's earlier and got some Valium for my nerves. Some examiners would say, 'I'm not even f***ing getting in the car with you.''

In a previous example of his driving abilities in December 2003, Ozzy severely injured himself during a quad bike ride on his estate in Chalfont St Peter, Buckinghamshire. The accident left Ozzy on a ventilator with a broken collarbone, eight broken ribs and a broken vertebra in his neck.

I Am Going To Tap On The Dashboard Once More...

Fred is taking his driving test. The examiner tells him, 'When I tap the dashboard I want you to show me what action you'd take if a child ran out in front of the car.' The examiner taps the dashboard, Fred throws the brakes on, winds down the window, and yells, 'Get out the way, you stupid little toe rag!'

Driving examiner: Tell me one way in which you could reduce the possibility of having an accident?
Learner driver: I could get myself so drunk I couldn't find my car keys.

Faults Most Commonly Exhibited During Driving Tests

Hazard procedure and cornering: Incorrect assessment. Poor safety margin. Unsystematic procedure. (78%)

Use of Gear: Late selection of gear. Intermediate gears not used to advantage. (72%)

Positioning: Straddling lanes. Incorrect positioning for right and left turns. (70%)

Braking: Late brake application. Harsh handbrake application. Braking and changing gear at the same time. (60%)

Distance observation: Late planning and assessment of traffic conditions. (58%)

Method of approach: Approaching too fast. Coasting to compulsory stops. Approaching offside at Keep Left sign. (48%)

Clutch control: Riding clutch. Letting clutch slip. Coasting. (48%)

Car sympathy: Not expressed in use of clutch, brakes and gears. (40%)

Gear changing: Harsh selection of gear. Changing down with relaxed accelerator. (38%)

Traffic observation: Poor anticipation. Late reaction. (38%)

Overtaking: Driving too close to other vehicle before overtaking. Overtaking on bends. Overtaking in face of approaching traffic. Cutting in again after overtaking. (38%)

Observation and obedience: Failing to remember signs when requested. Failing to conform to Stop signs and/or Keep Left signs. (36%)

Manoeuvring and reversing: Lacking judgement and control. (28%)

Correct use of speed: Using excessive speed in country lanes. Failing to make adequate progress in 70 mph areas. (26%)

Speed limits: Exceeding speed limits. (22%)

Steering: Releasing wheel. Crossing hands. (20%)

Restraint: Demonstrating insufficient restraint. (20%)

Maintaining adequate progress: Failing to maintain adequate progress when it was safe to do so. (14%)

Hand or mechanical signals: Giving late or misleading signals. (14%)

Correct use of horn: Failure to use horn when required. (14%)

Acceleration: Uneven acceleration. Poor sense of acceleration. (12%)

Obstructing other vehicles: Loitering at minor hazards. Cutting in. (8%)

Your Written Driving Test Commences Now!

Before you can take your practical driving test you need to pass your driving theory test. In the real test you are given a choice of answers. Some of these are right, and some are wrong. This is very confusing. Here are some of the actual questions asked in the proper test, but all the answers are wrong. Avoid these answers and you might have a chance of passing. Good luck!

In which of these situations should you avoid overtaking?
a) When you're drunk
b) When you're already doing 100 mph
c) When the car in front has its siren going
d) When you're the passenger

Before starting a journey it is wise to plan your route. How can you do this?
a) Ask Jeeves
b) Phone 999 and ask directions
c) Get a railway map and drive along the train line
d) Get a list of Little Chefs and keep stopping to ask where the next one is

You think the driver in the vehicle in front has forgotten to cancel his right indicator. You should:
a) Flash him and beep your horn
b) Wind down the window and call him an idiot
c) Overtake him and hope that he doesn't turn right anyway
d) Turn on your right indicator as well so he doesn't feel like he's the only idiot on the road

The fluid level in your battery is low. What should you top it up with?

a) Something battery, like a piece of cod
b) A pint of gold top
c) A pint of Carlsberg
d) Petrol

To avoid a collision when entering a contraflow system, you should:

a) Drive faster than everyone else
b) Drive slower than everyone else
c) Close your eyes so you don't get confused
d) Pray

If a trailer swerves or snakes when you are towing it you should

a) Jam on the brakes, knowing that if there's a collision it's the fault of the vehicle behind
b) Complain to the manufacturer
c) Swerve the car in unison with it
d) Ask Jeeves

A driver does something that upsets you. You should:

a) Immediately do something that upsets him right back
b) Screech to a halt, leap out of your car and kick his car
c) Phone the Samaritans
d) Have a couple of stiff whiskies and continue driving

You stop for pedestrians waiting to cross at a zebra crossing. They do not start to cross. What should you do?

a) Shout 'hurry up you morons!'
b) Take their names and addresses and report them to the police
c) Jump out of the car and punch them
d) Park the car in the middle of the crossing so they have to walk in the road and get run over

What should you do when overtaking a motorcyclist in strong winds?

a) Shout 'watch out greaseball!' when passing him
b) Poke a stick out of the passenger window to keep him at bay
c) Drive as close to him as possible so he doesn't have far to fall
d) Put 'Born to be Wild' on as loud as possible on the car stereo

Braking distances on ice can be

a) Quite long
b) Very long
c) As long as you want them to be
d) What's a braking distance?

How can you stop a caravan snaking from side to side?

a) Don't start the car
b) Put a lot of fat relatives in it
c) Remove the wheels before starting the journey
d) Drive at 3 mph

You are approaching a pelican crossing. The amber light is flashing. You must:

a) Try to not let it concern you
b) Report the faulty light to the police
c) Accelerate and try to get through before hitting a pedestrian
d) Quickly consult your highway code while attempting to keep one eye on the road

You are driving on an icy road. How can you avoid wheelspin?

a) Stop the car as quickly as possible
b) Attach sandpaper to the tyres
c) Buy a gritting lorry
d) Ask Jeeves

You must NOT sound your horn:
a) When passing a girl with a short skirt
b) At midnight on New Year's Eve
c) When passing another car displaying your football team's colours
d) Just because you are trapped inside and fear the car is going to go up in flames

You wish to park facing downhill. Which of the following should you do?
a) Work out which way is uphill and which way is downhill
b) Make sure your insurance is up to date
c) Make sure there is another car directly in front of you just in case
d) Tie a towrope to the bumper and then round a lamppost

Road humps, chicanes, and road narrowings are:
a) A flipping nuisance
b) Draconian impositions by a government hell-bent on banning private motor-car usage
c) Just a bit of fun dreamt up by local authorities
d) A complete waste of taxpayers' money and will be destroyed come the revolution

You are following a vehicle on a wet road. You should leave a time gap of at least
a) One second
b) One minute
c) One hour
d) No gap, because if there's no gap you can't crash

You are planning a long journey. Do you need to plan rest stops?
a) It all depends on how strong your bladder is
b) Not if you are on a diet as the motorway menus are just too tempting
c) No, rest stops are for wimps
d) Yes, you hardly want to do a long journey completely sober do you?

How should you dispose of a used battery?
a) Dump it in the nearest river
b) Donate it to a local school for them to have fun dismantling
c) Throw it on the fire
d) Take it back to the garage for a refund

Why should you always reduce your speed when travelling in fog?
a) So your vehicle emissions don't make the fog even worse
b) In case you're travelling on the wrong side of the road
c) Because you can't see where the speed cameras are
d) So the sat-nav lady can see where you're going

What percentage of all emissions does road transport account for?
a) 10%
b) 50%
c) 100%
d) Who cares?

You are at the scene of an accident. Someone is suffering from shock. You should:
a) Tell them to snap out of it
b) Get them to the nearest pub for a stiff drink
c) Nick their car
d) Say 'If you think you're in shock now mate, wait till you find that the other bloke's uninsured'

Motorcyclists will often look round over their right shoulder just before turning right. This is because:
a) All motorcyclists are right-handed
b) They're too tight to buy rear-view mirrors
c) They're worried they've just gone through a speed trap
d) They're paranoid about being followed

Overloading your vehicle can seriously affect the:
a) Road surface
b) Chances of taking anyone home tonight
c) Volume from your sound system
d) Space available for old take-away boxes, bottles, cans, fag packets etc

You are turning left on a slippery road. The back of your vehicle slides to the right. You should:
a) Look out for a giant magnet
b) Phone the manufacturer immediately and demand an explanation
c) Cross your fingers and hope for the best
d) Instruct all your passengers to heave to the left

Which two are badly affected if the tyres are under-inflated?
a) The local yobs' attempts to let your tyres down
b) The car's ability to float if there is flooding
c) Your chances of outdoing the cops in a chase
d) The income of your local garage's air machine

What is the most common cause of skidding?
a) Banana skins
b) Driving in a rubbish car
c) A badly mistimed sneeze
d) Driving while putting on make-up

Your mobile phone rings while you are travelling. You should:
a) Get into the fast lane where you can answer it with less traffic around you
b) Brake sharply – it could be important
c) Send the person a text saying you'll call them later
d) Steer with your knees until you've finished the call

You are in a one-way street and want to turn right. You should position yourself:
a) In the driving seat
b) In the 'crash' position
c) On the pavement – better safe than sorry
d) Behind someone else turning right – then you can blame them if it goes wrong

Catalytic converters are fitted to make the:
a) Headlights go green
b) Garage lots of money
c) Government lots of money
d) The car safe to transport your cat in

Which of the following may cause loss of concentration on a long journey?
a) Six cans of strong lager
b) A nudist colony's fun run
c) Another radio phone-in about the European Union
d) A speech by Gordon Brown

You are following a slow-moving vehicle on a narrow country road. There is a junction just ahead on the right. What should you do?
a) Tell the straw-sucking idiot to move over
b) Tell the straw-sucking idiot to turn right
c) Whizz round him as fast as possible and take the right
d) Set fire to the straw he's carrying on the vehicle and cause him to stop

Why are vehicles fitted with rear fog lights?
a) In case you need to reverse up a busy road in the fog
b) Because they look cool
c) In case of rear fog
d) To bump up the price of the car

An MOT certificate is normally valid for:
a) As long as your mate down the pub has done it for
b) Until your MOT breaks down
c) September 31st
d) What's an MOT?

What is the most likely cause of high fuel consumption?
a) Driving a lot
b) A leak in the petrol tank
c) Buying high fuel in the first place
d) Being a Formula One driver

You are waiting to emerge left from a minor road. A large vehicle is approaching from the right. You have time to turn, but you should wait. Why?
a) Because you're in the middle of a mobile phone call
b) It'll give you time to put your make-up on the mirror
c) The lorry driver might get the hump
d) Is this a trick question?

Motorcyclists are particularly vulnerable:
a) When displaying the insignia of the wrong Hell's Angels chapter in the wrong district
b) To wasps flying up their helmets
c) If bribed with a big fry-up
d) When doing wheelies at 110 mph on the motorway

You are approaching two cyclists. They approach a roundabout in the left-hand lane. In which direction should you expect the cyclists to go?

a) Who can read the mind of a cyclist?
b) Left? Right? Over the top of the roundabout? Who knows?
c) They may suddenly stop for a picnic for all I know
d) Never *expect* a cyclist to do anything vaguely logical

You see a vehicle coming towards you on a single-track road. You should:

a) Sound your horn and gesticulate until they reverse
b) Get out of the car and threaten dire consequences if they don't get out of the way
c) Just keep going and see who breaks first
d) Tell the driver you've got a problem with your reverse gear so he'll have to shift

At which type of crossing are cyclists allowed to ride across with pedestrians?

a) Cyclists do what they like don't they?
b) Have you ever seen a cyclist only do what they're allowed?
c) This question seems to imply that cyclists actually take notice of lights and all that stuff
d) I don't know, but if I need to find out I won't be asking a cyclist

On a three-lane motorway which lane should you normally use?

a) Oh, I wondered what those lines were for....
b) Whichever one's got least traffic in it
c) It's best to hedge your bets and straddle two lanes at once
d) The hard shoulder's usually nice and clear

How can you tell if you are driving on ice?
a) Look out of the window
b) Open the door and touch the road
c) You keep having to dodge skaters
d) You narrowly miss Torvill and Dean

You are driving along a country road. A horse and rider are approaching. What should you do?
a) Stop and give him a sugar lump
b) Stop and inform the rider that roads are for cars and fields are for horses
c) Check whether you've strayed onto a racecourse by mistake
d) Give a loud toot on your horn and drive past as quickly as possible

'Tailgating' means
a) Ogling women pedestrians
b) Being chased by a police car
c) Fitting wings to your car
d) Shutting the dog's tail in the boot door

When driving in falling snow you should
a) Stop to have a snowball fight with other motorists
b) Stop to take a picture before it's all churned up and slushy
c) Drive through red lights as most accidents are caused when people try to stop in snow
d) Slide the car down hills to save petrol

On very hot weather the road surface can become soft. Which two of the following will be most affected?
a) Pedestrians with bare feet
b) Dogs
c) Policemen on emergency point duty
d) Workmen who are trying to paint yellow lines on the surface (good!)

OTHER *!@&!%! DRIVERS

Patience is something you admire in the driver behind you and scorn in the one ahead.

Mac McCleary

Officially The World's Worst Driver

According to *Guinness World Records* the worst driver in history was a 75 year old man in McKinney, Texas. In 20 minutes on October 15, 1966 he received ten traffic tickets, drove on the wrong side of the road four times, committed four hit-and-run offences, and caused six accidents.

Ironically Texans are regularly ranked among the best drivers in the USA. Whether or not this is just in surveys conducted in Texas is not clear.

Have you ever noticed that anybody driving slower than you is an idiot, and anyone going faster than you is a maniac?

George Carlin

It Was The Other Driver's Fault!

Excuses Given By Drivers In Accident Insurance Claims

He should have known I wasn't looking in my blind spot.

I consider neither vehicle to blame, but if either was to blame it was the other one.

The other car shouldn't have been in my way.

He stopped too suddenly.

I don't know why he put his foot in the way while he was seeing me through the gap.

I looked both ways. He must have come out of nowhere really fast.

He must have been going way over the speed limit or I would have seen him.

It wasn't my fault. I did everything I was supposed to do.

The other car collided with mine, without giving any warning of its intentions.

If the other driver had stopped a few yards behind himself the accident would not have happened.

I'll bet she was putting on her makeup or something.

I'll bet he's drunk. He's got a sports car.

Road Rage

According to the myroadrage website one of the joint worst areas in the UK for bad driving is Greater London (along with Hampshire). It also reports that the colour car that features most in road rage incidents is black, and the second most common is silver. This wouldn't mean that the worst offenders are taxi drivers and hearses and the second worst were police cars, surely?

Stubborn Truckers

In a very narrow back street two trucks being driven in opposite directions meet. The two truck drivers are equally stubborn. Neither of them will give in to the other and reverse out of the way. And so they end up just sitting there angrily looking across at each other. Finally, one of them snatches up his tabloid newspaper and sits reading. At this point the other driver climbs out of his cab and walks slowly across to the other truck. He raps on the other driver's window and when it is wound down, he leans in and says, 'When you've finished the paper, could you bring it over to my truck so I can read it?'

USA Road Rage

Be careful where you go for your holidays and hire a car. In 2008 Miami was voted the worst road rage area for the third year running. Pittsburgh was judged to have the most courteous drivers. Prince Market Research also found that 43% of drivers reacted to bad driving by honking their horn, while 36% reacted by swearing. The other 21% presumably just went back home to Pittsburgh.

The elderly don't drive that badly; they're just the only ones with time to do the speed limit.

Jason Love

I'm Telling You, It Really Was The Other Driver's Fault!

More Excuses Given By Drivers In Accident Insurance Claims

I was driving along the motorway when the police pulled me over onto the hard shoulder. Unfortunately I was in the middle lane and there was another car in the way.

The other car collided with mine without giving me any warning of its intention.

I collided with a stationary lorry coming the other way.

A lorry backed through my windscreen into my wife's face.

I was unable to stop in time and my car crashed into the other vehicle. The driver and passengers then left immediately for a vacation with injuries.

I was backing my car out of the driveway in the usual manner, when it was struck by the other car in the same place it had been struck several times before.

No one was to blame for the accident but it would never have happened if the other driver had been more alert.

Could either driver have done anything to avoid the accident? Yes, they could have gone by bus.

I was going to work at 7 o'clock this morning and I drove out

of my drive straight into a bus. It wasn't my fault, the bus was 5 minutes early.

An invisible car came out of nowhere, struck my car and vanished.

On approaching the traffic lights the car in front suddenly broke.

The indirect cause of the accident was a little guy in a small car with a big mouth.

The first car stopped suddenly, the second car hit the first car and then a haggis ran into the back of the second car.

Motorway Madness
and Motorway Massage

In 1994 the Independent reported that a company called Pavillion Services was opening up a couple of massage centres for stressed motorists suffering from road rage. The so-called 'Road Rage Bays' were piloted at Forton near Lancaster and Hilton Park, Birmingham. They planned to extend the scheme if successful.

Three years later, in 1997, someone published the Motorway Massage Map, though this seems to have been more of a guide to massage parlours within easy reach of motorways rather than a sort of pit stop for nerve-jangled drivers. It included such delights as a massage parlour in Derby where the girls dressed as Euro 96 footballers, and one in Bradford that threw in a curry with the massage – though not literally one hopes.

Another Candidate
For World's Worst Driver

In 2008 it was reported that Canadian driver Gloria O'Neill had pleaded guilty to dangerous driving, driving while disqualified, driving with an invalid licence (which had itself been suspended numerous times since the 1980s) and failing to stop for police.

And this wasn't the first occasion Ms O'Neill had had car trouble.

Over the years she is said to have been involved in at least 15 collisions, often in rented or borrowed cars. Her licence was first suspended in 1978 when she was aged 21 and again in 1984 when she didn't pay a court judgment to the victim of a crash.

According to her parole documents she was once a drug addict who had become hooked on antidepressants and heroin following – can you guess – a car accident in 1995 during which she broke her back in two places. Following this accident, she had been charged with driving while under suspension and been given 15 days in jail.

With suspensions on two licences taken out under two different names by which she had been known at different stages in her life, she took out a third licence as Gloria O'Neill in 1998. In the course of two days in September 1999 she was involved in two crashes. In March and April 2000, she was involved in two separate collisions. In June 2000, she drove a rental car into the back of a bus and considered filing a lawsuit against the rental agency alleging faulty brakes. In November 2000 while driving without insurance, she hit a van and sent it careering into a bus shelter. In July and August 2001 she hit two more vehicles. In April 2002 she had another collision, two weeks later she hit the back of a Mercedes, in May she drove into the back of a parked car and two days later rear-ended an SUV.

Two weeks later she had another accident. Tragically, although somewhat inevitably, this time someone was killed. On May 27, 2002 O'Neill dragged a pedestrian, Salvatore Visicale, to his death on a crossing. When she was arrested following this accident, police discovered she was out on bail at the time for an outstanding fraud charge. She had driving suspensions on not one but two licences at the time.

She was given a ten-year driving ban (which it seems she didn't adhere to) and was sentenced to three years in prison but by March 2004, she was out on parole. Even following her latest conviction, the judge was reluctant to give her a lifetime driving ban and instead gave her a three year suspension presumably on the grounds that after this she will somehow have become a safe driver.

—————

The one thing that unites all human beings, regardless of age, gender, religion, economic status or ethnic background, is that, deep down inside, we ALL believe that we are above average drivers.

Dave Barry

Looking On The Bright Side

At a retirement home in Weybridge four old ladies are chatting.

The first one says, 'Ooh, I must get my cataracts done. I can hardly see to knit this pullover.'

'You're lucky,' says the second one. 'My arthritis is so bad I can hardly pick up my cup of tea.'

'You two think you've got it bad,' says the third old lady. 'I get these terrible dizzy spells and they're so bad I can hardly walk down the corridor most days.'

'Oh well,' says the fourth. 'Let's count our blessings. At least we can all still drive.'

You know, somebody actually complimented me on my driving today. They left a little note on the windscreen; it said 'Parking Fine.'

Tommy Cooper

Too bad all the people who know how to run the country are busy driving taxi cabs and cutting hair.

George Burns

There are two things no man will admit he cannot do well: drive and make love.

Stirling Moss

OTHER *!@&!%! ROAD USERS

I don't understand bus lanes. Why do poor people have to get to places quicker than I do?

Jeremy Clarkson

Horse Riders

Quite why a one horse-powered vehicle, i.e. a horse, would want to slug it out on the roads with gas-guzzlers, petrol heads, and assorted speed-freaks is anyone's guess, but they do, and then their rider trots them along at about eight miles an hour and you have to slow down so you don't scare the life out of them. The horse, that is, not the rider. We don't go zooming around their fields do we? Well not unless we've got a quad bike or something.

Cyclists

Oh, where do we start? They don't pay road tax, they don't have insurance, and when they go through a red light on the wrong side of the road and you knock them over it's your fault because you're a motorist. It wouldn't be so bad if they weren't so sanctimonious about saving the planet and all that but… (just gone for a lie down in a darkened room).

Tractors

They're even worse than horses for goodness sake. At least you can drive round a horse even if you do have to do it at 10 mph. But a tractor? You can't even see past it, let alone drive past it. They sit there in the middle of the road, laden with hay, or straw or some such other country cargo, blocking out your vision of the road ahead, and the driver sits about fifteen feet up in the air oblivious to all around (and especially behind) him and meanders along for miles without a care in the world. After a nerve-needling ten miles or so he decides he's going to go and annoy someone else and glory of glories, he indicates to turn off. Exhilarated with your new found freedom and a clear road, you put your foot down – only to be immediately nicked by a cop or a camera. Country life eh?

Americans are broad-minded people. They'll accept the fact that a person can be an alcoholic, a dope fiend, a wife beater, and even a newspaperman, but if a man doesn't drive, there is something wrong with him.

Art Buchwald

Motorcyclists

Anyone who can weave in and out of long queues of traffic while you have to sit silently fuming in your car has to be annoying. But at least they pay road tax.

Pedestrians

They shouldn't even be in the road. The clue is in the name, from the Latin *pedester*, meaning 'going on foot'. They have pavements, they have honorary pavements, known as crossings, to get across the road; they have underpasses, subways, bridges, and all manner of things to enable them to get from A to B without walking in the road, but do they use them? Well they might sometimes, but the rest of the time they're stepping out in front of you, playing 'dodge the truck' in the middle of the road, falling down drunk, rattling charity collection tins when you stop at the lights, trying to wash your windscreen, and generally being a pain in the neck. And they don't pay road tax either.

Ah...so many pedestrians, so little time...

Robin Williams

It Was The Pedestrian's Fault:

Yet More Excuses Given By Drivers In Accident Insurance Claims

The car in front hit the pedestrian but he got up so I hit him again.

A pedestrian hit me and went under my car.

The pedestrian was all over the road. I had to swerve a number of times before I hit him.

I was sure the old fellow would never make it to the other side of the road when I struck him.

The pedestrian had no idea which way to run as I ran over him.

I saw a slow moving, sad faced old gentleman as he bounced off the bonnet of my car.

I unfortunately ran over a pedestrian, and the old gentleman was taken to hospital, much regretting the circumstances.

The accident happened because I had one eye on the lorry in front, one eye on the pedestrian and one eye on the car behind.

The pedestrian ran for the pavement, but I still got him.

To avoid hitting the bumper of the car in front I struck a pedestrian.

I bumped into a lamppost which was obscured by human beings.

Three women were talking to each other and when two stepped back and one stepped forward I had to have an accident.

The accident was caused by me waving to the same man I hit last week.

I knocked over a man and he admitted it was his fault because he had been knocked down before.

How To Cross The Road

There is now an entire chapter in the *Highway Code* devoted to the subject of how to cross the road. However do not try reading it while actually attempting to cross the road or the results may be simultaneously tragic and ironic.

But hang on a minute!

Although drivers are expected to have read the Highway Code and abide its rules there is no such demand on pedestrians, yet they have an entire chapter telling them how to cross the road! And whoever knew just how complicated it could be? Not only do we have zebra crossings, we now have pelican crossings, puffin crossings and toucan crossings – a small menagerie. No wonder it needs a whole chapter.

And we haven't even mentioned equestrian crossings.

———

Walking isn't a lost art – one must, by some means, get to the garage.

Evan Esar

In-car entertainment

Things People Admit To Doing While Driving
According to a survey:

36 per cent of people admit to changing their clothes while driving

20 per cent said they liked to read the newspaper while driving

8 per cent admitted to shaving while driving

2 per cent said they liked to check their emails while driving.

Caravans

The whole point of driving in a car is to get somewhere else, but when you take a caravan with you you're going to end up in the same place – i.e. your caravan! It must be rather galling after driving 250 miles to think at last, we're there! And then return to the same old surroundings where you spent your last six holidays, not to mention your last dozen weekend breaks, and even your last few dozen lunch stops.

Yes, that same old narrow bed, seemingly designed for a stick insect, the same old Formica-topped table, the same chintzy curtains that don't quite fit the windows... still you could be getting all that in a b&b and paying for the privilege so maybe there is a point to it after all.

But when you go out on the road trailing a caravan behind your car you suddenly join the ranks of tractor-driving farmers, cyclists who insist on riding two abreast, and the rest of the most annoying people on the road. Even caravan owners probably don't like getting stuck behind caravans – especially when it's a bit breezy and the caravan in front is swaying from side to side like the back half of a pantomime horse.

There are almost half a million touring caravans on Britain's roads though it does probably seem like more when you're stuck behind a long line of them on the way to Penzance in mid-August. It may be no coincidence that the word 'caravan' also means a convoy. Though, in the caravanners' defence they do legally have to drive slower than cars. On motorways they're only allowed to do 60 mph, so spare a thought for the poor so and so's as you're bombing along at 85 mph and complaining about them.

I Knew I'd Lost Something

A man is driving along a quiet country road when he is stopped by a police patrolman.

'Excuse me sir,' says the policeman. 'Do you realise one of your rear indicators isn't working?'

'Oh no!' says the driver, seeming very shocked and surprised. 'I better have a look!'

So he jumps out of the car and follows the policeman to the back. He then breaks into tears and seems inconsolable.

'It's all right,' says the policeman. 'If you promise to get it fixed straight away, I won't nick you for it this time.'

'It's not that,' says the man, between sobs. 'I've lost my bloody caravan!'

Spooked

A woman is sitting in the back of a black cab when she suddenly realises she's reached her destination. She slides the glass screen across and taps the driver sharply on the shoulder, and says 'Hey, driver!'

The taxi driver almost jumps out of his skin and narrowly misses hitting a bus. He drives to the side of the road to calm himself down.

The woman apologises profusely. 'I'm sorry, I didn't realise it would scare you so much; I thought you'd be used to people doing that.'

'No, miss, this is my first day as a cab driver. I've been driving funeral hearses for the past thirty years.'

The Cost Is Deer

If you're a city driver you probably don't think about this very much, but every year 42,500 cars hit a deer. And he's getting pretty fed up with it. No, that's a very old joke, and we apologise for it unreservedly. But do you know what it will cost you if you hit a deer? £1,403.00. According to the AA that's the average cost per car, with the total annual cost at a staggering £59,000,000. Not only that, it could get worse. The deer population of the UK is currently 1,500,000, but it is rising. Either drivers are going to have to be a bit more careful or some of these deer are going to have to learn the green cross code.

Country Driving

A woman is driving along a country lane when she encounters a tractor being driven by a farmer. He refuses to give way and makes the woman back up to the next passing point. As he passes, the woman winds down her window and shouts, 'Pig!' The farmer swears at her and roars off round the corner, running over his prize pig.

It Was The Animal's Fault:

More Excuses Given By Drivers In Accident Insurance Claims

The horse came out of nowhere and landed on my car.

A cow wandered into my car. I was afterwards informed that the cow was half witted.

A bull was standing nearby and a fly must have tickled him because he gored my car.

In an attempt to kill a fly, I drove into a telephone pole.

I was thrown from the car as it left the road. I was later found in a ditch by some stray cows.

I knew the dog was possessive about the car but I would not have asked her to drive it if I had thought there was any risk.

I started to turn and it was at this point I noticed a camel and an elephant tethered at the side of the road. This distraction caused me to lose concentration and I hit a bollard.

I started to slow down but the traffic was more stationary than I thought it was.

I was driving along when I saw two kangaroos copulating in the middle of the road causing me to ejaculate through the sun-roof.

Carversation

Do you chat to your Passat? Have you muttered to your Metro? Would you converse with a hearse? A survey conducted by the motors.co.uk website in October 2009 found that nearly half the drivers in the UK talk to their cars. When they say 'talk', do they actually mean 'swear'?

The survey found that 44% of drivers spoke to their car some of the time while 31% spoke to their car all the time. All the time? Don't they let the car get a word in edgeways occasionally? Haven't they seen Knight Rider? Don't they have radios to listen to?

According to the survey 25% of people never spoke to their car. They, presumably, are the people who are constantly on their mobile phones while at the wheel.

Strangely, the same survey also found that 26% percent of drivers had a pet name for their car. 26%? Wait a minute! This means that 5% of drivers are talking to their car 'all the time' and they don't even know the car's name!

Did The Air Bag Move For You?

In April 2009 it was reported that a 28-year-old man and his 22-year-old girlfriend had been caught by police in Norway having sex in their Mazda 323. Unfortunately the car was travelling along a motorway at 133 kph at the time. And not only were they having sex in a moving vehicle, they were breaking the motorway's 100 kph speed limit as well.

According to police superintendent Tor Stein Hagen the car was veering from one side of the road to the other, the driver's view of the road being obscured by his girlfriend. Superintendent Tor Stein Hagen informed the world's press that the driver's female companion had been sitting on his lap 'while he was driving and doing the act, shall we say.'

According to the police the driver was due to receive a fine of 'several thousand Norwegian crowns' and a lengthy driving ban.

My wife wants sex in the back of the car and she wants me to drive.

Rodney Dangerfield

I Had A Severe Bout
Of Diarrhoea And Had
To Speed To A Public Toilet

This classic excuse was genuinely given by Manchester United manager Sir Alex Ferguson when he was apprehended illegally driving on the hard shoulder of the M602 in Eccles, Greater Manchester in February 1999.

Bury Magistrates were told that Sir Alex had been suffering from severe diarrhoea at the time of the incident. This was undoubtedly true because his story was backed up by Mike Stone who was coincidentally club doctor for Manchester United. After a consultation with Dr Stone, Sir Alex took some tablets which temporarily made him feel better. On his way home however he began to suffer stomach cramps and had an urgent need to visit the lavatory. This would have been bad enough but at the time the M602 in Eccles was rather more congested than Sir Alex's insides were feeling.

And so to avoid queuing, he drove onto the hard shoulder in an attempt to get back to the comfort of the toilets at Manchester United's Old Trafford stadium. Sir Alex's defence lawyer claimed he had faced two options after being caught in the traffic jam. One of these was claimed to be 'unthinkable' and the other was 'to take evasive action.'

Presumably it was a genuine excuse. Well, Sir Alex always looks like he's suffering doesn't he?

Fluffy Dice

According to legend the fashion for hanging fluffy, furry or fuzzy dice dates back to the US hot-rod culture in the years immediately following the Second World War.

During the war US pilots supposedly used dice as good luck charms during flying missions. They would place a pair of dice with sevens showing on their instrument panels.

The pilots returned after the war and carried on the habit in their cars rather than their planes.

And thus over-size novelty pairs of fluffy dice to hang from your rear view mirror eventually evolved – allegedly.

Alf says he's got a stereo system in his car. His wife in the passenger seat and her mother in the back.

Purrfect

A man misses the last bus home and as he starts to walk a car stops and the driver offers him a lift. He notices that there is a cat on the front seat in a basket so he sits in the back.

As they drive along he begins to notice that when the cat swishes its tail to the left the man turns left and when it swishes it to the right he turns right.

He thinks it must be a coincidence but after it keeps on happening he just has to say something.

'Excuse me mate,' he says, 'I couldn't help but notice, but is that cat giving you directions?'

'Yeah, 'course.' Say the driver, 'It's the latest gadget – cat nav.'

I have an answering machine in my car. It says, 'I'm home now. But leave a message and I'll call when I'm out.'

Steven Wright

The A1 number plate

Although the A1 car registration plate was not the first in the world, this first British car number plate has a huge cachet because of its pleasing numerical simplicity.

When the requirement to display a car registration plate became enshrined in British law in 1903 some individuals saw the significance of owning the A1 plate and queued all night to obtain it. First in the queue was philosopher Bertrand Russell's brother, Earl Russell. Surprisingly, after all his efforts to obtain it he owned it for just three years, selling the Napier car and the plate in 1906 to the Chairman of London County Council. The coveted plate adorned many different cars over the years, and was owned by many different people and organisations, including Dunlop Ltd until in 2000 it was sold to the Sultan of Brunei's brother, Prince Jeffrey of Brunei. At the same time as he bought this famous plate he also bought the 1A number plate. These were proudly fitted to his pair of identical white Bentley Azure cars, and may not be up for sale again anytime soon.

Pimp my ride

I replaced the headlights in my car with strobe lights, so it looks like I'm the only one moving.

Steven Wright

174

MAG 1C or TR4G 1C?

Having your very own personalised number plate may be the ultimate in status or the ultimate in naffness, depending on which way you look at it. As the ultimate in high status number plates, A1, is now off the market for the time being at least, you may have to be a bit more inventive in what registration plate you choose. Cherished plates, or, as the Americans less kindly know them, vanity plates, are still big business, and of course, some of the best ones have been nabbed by rich celebrities. In the 1960s Jimmy Tarbuck bought the ultimate comedian's number plate, COM 1C, and celebrity hairdresser Nicky Clarke invested in H41 RDO, which, if you squint a bit and use your imagination, becomes 'hairdo'. Magician Paul Daniels conjured up MAG 1C, while David Beckham has the rather unimaginative DB7 – couldn't he afford DB1? Actually, the DB not only stood for David Beckham, but also for the DB7 Aston Martin to which the footballer had it attached.

Cross-dressing comic Danny La Rue once owned the rather provocative RU12, which would have worked better with a question mark at the end, while current soccer celeb Wayne Rooney has the laddish WAZ 8 which presumably isn't a reference to his erstwhile IQ.

But perhaps the ultimate in number plate cool has to be that of the Queen. No, she doesn't have HRH 1 or QU 33N or even L1Z, she simply doesn't have a number plate at all as her official limousines are not required to display registration plates. How status-tastic is that?

But apart from desirable number plates, we have what could be termed the undesirable ones; i.e. those which spell out unpleasant, smutty or derogatory names or words. In 2009 the DVLA had to drop from auction two number plates which were felt to be offensive to gay people: F4 GOT and D1 KES. The DVLA (or should that be DVL4?) has already taken certain number plates from circulation, including 054MA, which could be interpreted as the first name of a certain Mr Bin Laden, HE58 0LA (Hezbollah), and combinations such as J1H4D (Jihad). Though strangely, some controversial plates seem to have slipped through the net, e.g. N4 KED, NUD9 E, and 701 LET, which can just about be read as 'toilet' if the wind's blowing in the right direction.

But personalised plates can be expensive. In February 2009 the number plate 1 HRH was sold for £113, 815. The bidder was anonymous, but was surely not Her Majesty. Harry Hill perhaps? The owner of Chelsea FC, Roman Abramovich paid £285,000 for VIP 1 but that pales into insignificance compared to the reported £7,000,000 paid by a Middle eastern businessman for the licence plate '1'.

Some record-busting prices recently paid for must-have plates are:

£440,625 for F1

£404,062 for S1

£331,500 for M1

£258.775 for G11

£254,000 for 51 NGH (Singh, geddit?)

£247,652 for 1RH

£231,000 for K1 NGS

£197,000 for 100

£130,00 for 6B

£101,050 for MR51 NGH (a bargain for the far more polite version of the above 51 NGH)

And a mere £79,314 for the rather neat RU55 ELL

No Registration –
It Could Be One Of Two People!

In the UK there is one other person apart from the Queen who has the privilege of driving without number plates: the Lord High Commissioner to the General Assembly of the Church of Scotland. And he's only allowed to do this for one week each year during the annual Assembly. I bet he spends the time speeding around because he knows Her Majesty will get any speeding camera fines through the post.

More Celebrity
Personalised Number Plates

1 KO	Boxer Chris Eubank
1 TEL	El Tel, Terry Venables
B17CH X	Woman's boxing champion, Cathy Brown
CHU 88	Fishing enthusiast Chris Tarrant
DS 500	Former Liberal Party leader, Lord David Steel
MRD 1Y	TV handyman Tommy Walsh
ORV 1L	Yes it's Keith Harris and his one named driver, Orville
RA1	Lord Richard Attenborough
S8 RRY	An apologetic Robbie Williams

Did you know: Roman Abramovich's VIP1 number plate was previously used on Pope John Paul II's Pope-mobile during a papal visit to Ireland.

World's Worst
Personalised Number Plates

8OTOX

M9CHO

B1G B4LL5

AR51 OLE

UB6 1B9

PB4 UGO

W11 W11

OSH 1T

BEMYHO

U NV ME

2B & NOT 2B (on a pair of Bentleys)

The Wonderful World
Of Bumper Stickers

I Brake For No Apparent Reason.

If you can read this, I can hit my brakes and sue you.

If you can read this I have lost my caravan.

A.A.A.A.A. – An organization for drunks who drive.

Give me ambiguity or give me something else.

A fool and his money are a girl's best friend.

I'd give my right arm to be ambidextrous.

Don't follow me, I'm lost too!

Without geometry, life is pointless.

Baby on board – there's no room in the car.

If you're rich, I'm single.

Lose 10 pounds of ugly fat – cut off your head!

Learner driver – please feel free to shout abuse.

Vote Labour – it's easier than working!

Don't drink and drive...You might hit a bump and spill your drink.

Caution ! I Drive The Same Way You Do!

I may be slow but at least I'm in front of you.

Love may be blind, but marriage is a real eye opener.

If at first you don't succeed, call it version 1.0!

I don't suffer from insanity. I enjoy every minute of it.

I'm not as you think as you drunk I am.

I took an IQ test and the results were negative.

He who laughs last thinks slowest!

Rebuilt with genuine stolen parts.

Death is life's way of telling you you've been fired.

Hard work has a future payoff. Laziness pays off now.

Honk If You Want To See My Finger.

My Granddad's other car is a hearse.

The more people I meet, the more I like my dog.

You Think Next Door's
4 x 4 Is Big?!

Jay Ohrberg of Burbank, California is a car collector and builder who runs Jay Ohrberg Star Cars. Jay's Star Cars is a car hire firm with a difference. It offers a vast array of models from TV and film including various Batmobiles, the Flintstones car, Chitty Chitty Bang Bang, Herbie the *Love Bug*, the *Knight Rider* car, the *Munsters* car, the *A Team*'s van… you get the idea!

Jay also owns American Dream which *Guinness World Records* says is the world's longest car. American Dream is a 100-foot limousine including a king-size waterbed, a Jacuzzi, a sun deck, a king sized bed and a swimming pool complete with diving board. The car has two drivers' compartments (one at each end of the vehicle to help with reversing).

And in case you're thinking 100 feet is quite a long way to walk from one end of the car to the other, the vehicle also has its very own helicopter landing pad.

Strange Customs

Richie is a spoilt brat, and when he reaches seventeen his father buys him a Bentley.

He proudly takes it out to show off to his friends and they're all impressed apart from Tarquin.

'Oh it's all very well Richie,' says Tarquin, 'but my old Ford's got a fridge. Has your Bentley got a fridge?'

'Er, well, no,' says Richie, rather embarrassed in front of his friends. So next day he goes and gets a fridge fitted.

Next time he sees his friends he tells Tarquin he's now got a fridge in his car.

Tarquin isn't impressed however and tells Richie that he not only has a fridge in his old Ford, but that he has a home cinema screen too.

So Richie goes out and gets one of a screen fitted in his car as well and the next time he sees his friend he informs him of the fact.

'Hmm, not bad,' says Tarquin, 'but I've now had a bed fitted in my car.'

Tarquin is so annoyed he immediately goes and gets a bed fitted in his Bentley.

That night, he's out driving when he sees Tarquin's old Ford parked in a lay-by.

He is so keen to prove to him that he's got all the latest gadgets and fittings that he stops the Bentley, gets out of the car and knocks on the tinted windows of the old Ford.

'Hey Tarquin!' he shouts. 'Come out and have a look at this! I've got a bed in my car as well now.'

There is a pause, before the window lowers down and Tarquin, who is naked and has wet hair, looks out angrily and exclaims, 'You got me out of the shower just to tell me that?!'

I AM THE PASSENGER

Most cars on our roads have only one occupant, usually the driver.
Carol Malia (BBC Presenter)

Kids In Cars

All parents will know the problems of keeping young children amused on long car journeys. You get them to spot animals such as sheep, cows, or horses; you tell them to count how many yellow cars they see, or how many tractors; you get them to look for words on car number plates, or unusual road signs. The tried and trusted games that have kept children quiet on long car journeys for decades. We've all done it, but why not update it a bit? The modern world has so many more possibilities for kids' games in cars.

Never have more children than you have car windows.
Erma Bombeck

Old game	New game
Seeing how many cows you can spot	Seeing how many speed traps you can spot and stop dad getting nicked
Counting sheep and hoping it will make them go to sleep (the kids, not the sheep)	Counting traffic cones and being virtually assured they'll drop off
Thinking up jokes and riddles	Thinking up excuses for when you're stopped by the police
Looking out for tractors	Looking out for motorway delay announcements
Playing I Spy	Playing I Spy A Speed Camera
Playing 'Guess Who I Am?'	Playing 'Guess which child will need a toilet stop first?'
Looking for funny car number plates	Looking for funny drivers swerving all over the road as they talk on their mobiles

Back Seat Drivers

You're going too fast! Watch that cyclist! Don't forget to indicate! Have you got Your lights on? Whenever one of those back seat drivers tells you where to go you feel like telling them where to go, but usually you can't. Probably because it's your mother-in-law or your mother, or your partner, or your driving instructor or something.

The other temptation is to say, 'OK, if you're so clever, why don't you drive then?'

But the odd thing is that quite often these back seat drivers can't actually drive themselves. It's like that old saying: 'Those who can, do; those who can't, teach.'

This should now be adapted to: 'Those who can, drive; those who can't, drive the driver round the twist with their constant nagging, and general pain in the backside wittering.'

The other thing about back seat drivers is that they're not always in the back seat, they're often in the front passenger seat where they are in a perfect position to suddenly stick their arm in front of your face and point to some real or imagined hazard that they think you haven't noticed.

Of course the only way you can get your own back is when you hire a minicab. You can then be the back seat driver from hell, constantly telling the driver where he's going wrong, where he should be going and a thousand and one other things. And, because he's hoping to get a tip at the end of the journey he'll just have to lump it.

Oh, we're all back seat drivers given half the chance. Mainly because we know best and all other drivers on the road are idiots.

Did you ever notice when you blow in a dog's face he gets mad at you? But when you take him in a car he sticks his head out the window.

Steve Bluestone

A man is driving fast down the motorway when he is stopped by a police patrolman.

'Excuse me sir,' says the policeman. 'Didn't you notice? About two miles back your wife fell out of the car.'

'Did she?' said the man, sounding relieved, 'And there I was thinking I'd suddenly gone deaf.'

My wife isn't very bright. The other day she was at the store, and just as she was heading for our car, someone stole it! I said, 'Did you see the guy that did it?' She said, 'No, but I got the licence plate.'

Rodney Dangerfield

Hitchhikers

Why would anyone pick up a hitchhiker? A hitchhiker is someone who not only can't afford his own car, he can't even afford a ticket for a train or a coach. A hitchhiker, therefore, is someone with no money. What likelier person is there who's going to rob you?

When you're driving your car is your home. Would you invite a complete stranger – complete with muddy boots and personal hygiene issues into your house? Imagine it – you're sitting watching TV one night and someone knocks on your door and says, 'Hello. You don't know me, but can I come in and be your guest for the next two or three hours, eat your all extra-strong mints, emit unpleasant bodily odours and make awkward conversation until we're both embarrassed and look out of separate windows in silence for the rest of the time?

'Oh, and by the way, I haven't had a bath for four days, and I might be an axe murderer.'

Some drivers must get very lonely on the road. There's no other explanation for it.

Mad Cow

A woman is driving along a country road when a farmer thumbs a lift. He looks harmless enough, but when she offers him a lift he leads a cow out from the nearby field.

'Er, excuse me,' says the woman, 'there's no way I'm having that cow in the car.'

'No, that's OK,' says the farmer, 'I'll just tie her to the bumper, she can trot along behind.'

So off they go at thirty miles an hour with the cow running along behind. After a while the woman speeds up to forty, then fifty miles an hour. The cow is still running behind. Then they get onto the motorway, and get up to sixty, seventy, then eighty miles an hour. The cow is still running behind for all it is worth.

The woman looks in the mirror and sees that the cow has its tongue sticking out.

'Is your cow OK?' asks the woman. 'She's got her tongue sticking out.'

'Is it sticking out to the left or to the right?' asks the farmer.

'To the right,' replies the woman.

'Oh, you know what that means don't you?' says the farmer.

'No, what?'

'She's trying to overtake.'

THE ROAD GOES
EVER ONWARD

Everything in life is somewhere else, and you get there in a car.

E. B. White

The Worst Gridlock in the World

Everyone naturally believes that the worst gridlock in the world occurs in their own town, and more specifically, on their own regular journey to work.

The good news is that someone's got it worse than you!

In 2008 allworldcars.com came up with a list of the twenty worst traffic jam cities in the world, and there was only one British city in the entire list. No prizes for guessing that it was London. Others included Tokyo, Los Angeles and Bangkok.

In the sme year *Time* magazine reported that Sao Paolo in Brazil had the world's worst traffic jams where a journey of just one block could take two hours. They also said that a thousand new vehicles were taking to the city's roads *every day*, so things can only get worse! There. You think you've got problems?

The Longest Tailback Ever

It has been reported that the longest tailback ever was on February 16, 1980 when a traffic queue between Paris and Lyon was 109 miles. This was due to 'bad weather' and 'many cars'. Yes, without those pesky cars it wouldn't have been very impressive at all.

Longest Car Journey Ever

Guinness World Records features Emil and Liliana Schmid who have travelled 398,369 miles in their Toyota Land Cruiser since 1984, taking in 162 different countries and territories. Just as well they didn't start four years earlier, or they might have ended up in that Paris-Lyon tailback and still been there now.

Why do they call it rush hour when nothing moves?
                                        Robin Williams (from Mork and Mindy)

Life is too short for traffic.

                                                                Dan Bellack

Each year it seems to take less time to fly across the ocean and longer to drive to work.

                                                                Anonymous

If you're in a car with a man and he stops and asks for directions, listen carefully, because he won't, and it will be your fault if you get lost.

                                                                Rita Rudner

Remember: He who hesitates is not only lost, but miles from the next exit.

Men can read maps better than women, 'cause only the male mind could conceive of one inch equalling a hundred miles.

Rosanne Barr

Men are superior to women. For one thing they can urinate from a speeding car.

Will Durst

Two wrongs don't make a right, but three lefts do.

Jason Love

The Worst In Europe

In December 2009 the Commission For Integrated Transport said in a report that Britain has the most congested roads in Europe. They said that the average British worker takes 46 minutes to commute to work in the car while the average Italian only takes 23 minutes. Surely that couldn't be anything to do with the Italians driving like maniacs could it?

Mass transportation is doomed to failure in North America because a person's car is the only place where he can be alone and think.

Marshall McLuhan

Doctor Who and the Tardiness

But all this pales into insignificance when you look at the traffic problems to come in the future. A 2007 episode of *Doctor Who*, entitled Gridlock, imagined New York (or New New York to be precise) in the year 5,000,000,053 where a journey of ten miles can take six years. If this happened in Britain it would mean that you could set off on your seventeenth birthday just after passing your driving test and get say from London to Brighton before you reached 50. A stroll along the promenade and a candy floss and you would be back home in plenty of time to celebrate your 80th. Still perhaps by then we'll all have a Tardis to circumvent such inconveniences.

No Direction Home

Julie and her husband move into their new house and invite her mother Ethel over for Sunday dinner. The only problem is that Ethel has to go on the motorway for the first time in her life at the age of 74. Julie is a bit worried, but Ethel insists that she'll be fine.

'All right, Mum,' says Julie, 'if you're sure, but if you get into any difficulties just give me a ring from your mobile.'

Mum agrees and sets off in plenty of time to get there for lunch.

Just as Julie is putting the Sunday joint in the oven she hears a traffic report on the radio announcing, 'Police have been called to the M6 where a car is driving in the wrong direction against the oncoming traffic causing panic and confusion.'

Julie immediately phones her mum on the mobile to warn her.

'Mum, I'm just phoning to say be careful. I've just heard on the radio that there's a car on the motorway driving in the wrong direction.'

'I know, love,' replies her mum, 'and it's not just one car – there's hundreds of them!'

Road signs

Did you know that on the A128 there's a big sign reading 'secret nuclear bunker', and an arrow pointing to where it is? Duh... Still at least they haven't got the Russian translation underneath.

The Magic Roundabout

It's slightly disconcerting to be driving along a road in an unfamiliar area and suddenly finding a sign pointing to *The Magic Roundabout*. Have you entered a parallel universe? Are you losing your marbles? Did someone at Little Chef drop a hallucinogenic drug in your coffee? No, you have probably just reached Swindon, where this five-for-the-price-of-one traffic feature, once jokingly called the Magic Roundabout, is now officially called by this name.

Thoughts of encountering Dougal, Florence, Dylan and Zebedee are suddenly forgotten as you traverse what the BBC once called 'one of the ten scariest roundabouts in the UK', and one car magazine elevated to 'one of the world's worst junctions.' One wonders whether three of the others are also in the UK, because High Wycombe, Hemel Hempstead and Colchester all have their very own Magic Roundabouts. Time for bed, or time to party?

The World's Widest Road

The Monumental Axis is a central avenue in Brazil's capital Brasília. It is believed to be the world's widest road with space for 160 cars to drive side by side. I bet there's always someone hogging lane 81 though.

The car has become the carapace, the protective and aggressive shell, of urban and suburban man.

Marshall McLuhan

And that just shows you how important the car is in Formula One Racing.

Murray Walker